MW01394246

B   9408
SCA
Carson, Glenn Thomas
   Calling out the called

FIRST BAPTIST CHURCH
P. O. BOX 2145
HARLINGEN, TEXAS 78551

CALLING OUT THE CALLED

The Life and Work of Lee Rutland Scarborough

By
Glenn Thomas Carson

Foreword By
H. Leon McBeth

EAKIN PRESS ★ Austin, Texas

FIRST EDITION

Copyright © 1996
By Glenn Thomas Carson

Published in the United States of America
By Eakin Press
An Imprint of Sunbelt Media, Inc.
P.O. Drawer 90159 ★ Austin, TX 78709-0159

ALL RIGHTS RESERVED. No part of this book may be reproduced in any form without written permission from the publisher, except for brief passages included in a review appearing in a newspaper or magazine.

2   3   4   5   6   7   8   9

ISBN 1-57168-018-7

Library of Congress Cataloging-in-Publication Data

Carson, Glenn Thomas.
   Calling out the called : the life and work of Lee Rutland Scarborough / by Glenn Thomas Carson : foreword by H. Leon McBeth. — 1st ed.
     p.   cm.
   Includes bibliographical references and index.
   ISBN 1-57168-018-7
   1. Scarborough, L. R. (Lee Rutland), 1870–1945.   2. Baptists — United States — Clergy — Biography.   3. Southern Baptist Convention — Clergy — Biography.
   4. Evangelists — United States — Biography.   I. Title.
BX6495.S37C37   1995
286'.1'092–dc20
[B]
                                                    95-35692
                                                     CIP

*To Leslie,
with whom I share my calling*

Lee Rutland Scarborough

Contents

Foreword by H. Leon McBeth ... vii
Introduction ... ix
Acknowledgments ... xiii

Chapter 1 Becoming Baptist ... 1
    Family Heritage and Home Life ... 2
    Life in West Texas ... 3
    Parental Influence ... 5
    The Cowboy Years ... 7
    The School Years ... 8
    Transformation and Divine Call ... 12
    Pastoral Experience ... 14
    Summary ... 20

Chapter 2 Building a Seminary ... 22
    B. H. Carroll's Dream ... 23
    The Chair of Fire ... 25
    Move to Fort Worth ... 27
    Location and Building ... 28
    Spring Bible Conference ... 29
    From Professor to President ... 31
    Scarborough's Inauguration ... 33
    Transfer of Ownership ... 34
    Financial Matters ... 35
    Final Years ... 41
    Conflict with J. Frank Norris ... 42
    Orthodoxy in Academia ... 43
    Denominationalism vs. Independence ... 46
    The Fruits of Norrisism ... 48
    Summary ... 50

Chapter 3 Creating Something New ... 52
    Convention Structure ... 53
    1919 Convention ... 54

	Campaign Commission	56
	Campaign Strategy	58
	Campaign Publicity	61
	Campaign Activity	64
	Victory Week	66
	Campaign Follow-up	67
	Conservation Commission	70
	Results of the Campaign	72
	New Denominationalism	73
	Cooperative Program	76
	Summary	77
Chapter 4	Giving a New Direction	80
	A New Thrust in Evangelism	82
	Calling Out the Called	85
	Evangelistic Teaching in the Classroom	88
	A Model for Evangelism	90
	The New Testament and Evangelism	91
	Strategies for Evangelism	92
	Goal of Evangelism	94
	Evangelistic Themes in Writing	94
	Personal Evangelism	97
	Church Evangelism	99
	Summary	100
Chapter 5	Thinking Through It All	102
	Analysis of a Denominationalist	102
	Evaluation of the New Denominationalism	106
Appendix A:	Lee Rutland Scarborough: A Chronology	111
Appendix B:	Scarborough's Statement of Faith	112
Appendix C:	Letter from J. Frank Norris	115
Appendix D:	The Fruits of Norrisism	120
Notes		133
Bibliography		151
Index		159

Foreword

The story of L. R. Scarborough is worth telling, and Glenn Carson has told that story well. This book will appeal not only to historians, but also to people with an interest in the early social and religious development in Texas.

With a sure step, Carson retraces the life story of Lee Rutland Scarborough, hard-riding cowboy from a pioneer West Texas ranch family. Young Scarborough graduated from Baylor University and was greatly influenced by B. H. Carroll during his time there. He then entered Yale Law School to pursue his life dream to be a lawyer. However, a sense of divine calling turned him toward the ministry instead.

Very few people have done more to shape Southern Baptists in the twentieth century than did Scarborough. When B. H. Carroll founded the Southwestern Baptist Theological Seminary in Fort Worth in 1908, he persuaded young Scarborough, then pastor of First Baptist Church in Abilene, to become the first professor of evangelism. This "Chair of Fire," as Carroll called the new professorship, helped establish evangelism as an academic study as well as an evangelical practice in American theological education.

Over the years Scarborough also helped shape a new concept of cooperative denominationalism among Southern Baptists. As Dr. Carson points out, this is nowhere more evident than in Scarborough's leadership in the "75 Million Campaign," which established the unique method of raising and disbursing Southern Baptist funds. Though many will remember Scarborough in connection with evangelism, Carson shows that he was also a primary architect for new forms of denominational cooperation.

Scarborough also helped raise the money to start the Southwestern Seminary, led in the selection of the building site in south Fort Worth, and oversaw construction of the first building. It is little wonder that in 1915 he succeeded Carroll as president.

Scarborough was the Seminary's second president and served until 1942, the longest tenure of any Southwestern president.

The Seminary still bears the marks of Scarborough's leadership. Significant buildings bear his name, and the Scarborough Institute of Church Growth perpetuates his influence in evangelism and church growth.

Dr. Carson combines solid scholarship with an excellent writing style to tell the story of this important figure in Texas religious history. The book is based on thorough and meticulous research, but the author does not overlook human interest details in the story. Well-chosen examples and quotations from Scarborough's colorful life spice up the pages and keep the reader turning pages. The real man, Lee Scarborough, is revealed in these pages.

Glenn Thomas Carson has credentials to write this book. He received his Ph.D. in Church History from Southwestern Seminary in 1992. He has presented papers at a number of scholarly society meetings and has published articles in several popular as well as academic journals. A popular speaker and teacher, Dr. Carson has taught Church History at both Southwestern Seminary and Charleston Southern University in South Carolina.

We will hear more from Dr. Carson in the future. This first book has established him as one of the most promising young historians in America today.

        H. Leon McBeth
        Distinguished Professor of Church History
        Southwestern Baptist Theological Seminary
        Fort Worth, Texas

Introduction

L. R. Scarborough was a cowboy. Growing up on a West Texas ranch, it was the only thing he ever dreamed of being. Horses, the cattle round-up, and roping were the images of his boyhood and, quite frankly, he liked it that way. He was at home in the saddle and that was where he intended to stay. Becoming a world-renowned Baptist leader was the farthest thing from this young Texan's mind.

But that's exactly what happened.

Perhaps Lee Rutland Scarborough (1870–1945) is best remembered as the second president of Southwestern Baptist Theological Seminary. Had his contribution to Southern Baptists stopped there it would have been no mean achievement. However, his accomplishments did not end at the foot of Seminary Hill. Instead, he rose to the very top of Southern Baptist leadership responsibilities. Indeed, Scarborough became one of the most prominent Baptists in the world during the first half of the twentieth century.

The legacy of L. R. Scarborough lives today in the forms of Southern Baptist organization in particular and Baptist evangelism in general. He led Southern Baptists into a new era of convention structure with the methods forged in the very successful 75 Million Campaign. Operating from 1919 through 1924, with Scarborough as general director, this campaign served as the forerunner and model for the Southern Baptist Cooperative Program. It was a brand new kind of organization for Southern Baptists. The 75 Million Campaign and the Cooperative Program forever changed the way Southern Baptists gathered and distributed funds. It was a new structure. Indeed, it was a "New Denominationalism" and L. R. Scarborough was at the heart of this movement.

Scarborough's New Denominationalism also included a

renewed emphasis on and fresh strategy for evangelism. As the holder of the world's first professorship in evangelism, Scarborough was uniquely suited to lead Southern Baptists into a new type of evangelism—one that centered in what he named "Calling Out the Called." His watershed work *Recruits for World Conquests*[1] served as a trumpet blast to enlist young men and women in vocational Christian service. When the Sunday School Board reprinted 25,000 copies of the book during the 75 Million Campaign, more than 6,000 people accepted the vocational call.[2] It was a new era for Southern Baptists and a New Denominationalism envisioned by L. R. Scarborough.

Scarborough's is a story begging to be told. From cowboy to Yale graduate to Seminary president in one lifetime was a long way to go. But through it all was the strong sense of calling. His father, George W. Scarborough, was a Baptist minister—part of the time anyway. Even though he earned his livelihood in Texas as a rancher, the elder Scarborough saw his real job as preaching. He was called. And from the very beginning Lee Scarborough knew what it meant to be called.

But when he finally came into his own as a Southern Baptist leader, L. R. Scarborough took the idea of calling one step further. For him, to be called was only the first level of Christian service. To *call out* the called was the more advanced level. He believed that every person in the ministry was called to the task by God himself. Yet, he also believed that God allowed other Christians the privilege of being involved in the process of calling. The "called," then, became a vital link in calling others to similar service for the church.

Called and *calling* are words to describe Scarborough's whole approach to his work. He considered himself to be divinely called, and every aspect of his career was somehow connected to calling others.

Until I wrote my dissertation on Scarborough in 1992, no extensive historical research had been attempted into his life. H. E. Dana's *Lee Rutland Scarborough: A Life of Service*, published in 1942, was previously the only monograph which chronicled Scarborough's life and ministry.[3] Now over fifty years old, Dana's book serves as a tribute to a personal and esteemed friend. It is an inspiring work to read, but can in no way be considered a critical look at Scarborough. However, it does provide source material which may not exist elsewhere. Dana quotes frequently from a transcript of Scarborough's dictations to his secretary. In these passages, Scarborough recalls intimate details of his home life, conversion, and call to ministry. It is an up-close and exclusive look into Scarborough's most treasured memories.

Scarborough himself produced numerous books and articles which serve as source material. His books range from the very practical, like *Prepare to Meet God*;[4] to the devotional, like *Holy Places and Precious Promises*;[5] and even to the historical in *A Modern School of the Prophets*,[6] which tells the story of Southwestern Seminary. Newspaper articles by Scarborough are also available, which give a personal view of his work.

Along the way I will analyze and evaluate what I call Scarborough's "New Denominationalism." How did it affect the Southern Baptist Convention? What were the results of Scarborough's financial and evangelistic efforts? How did the ministry of L. R. Scarborough change the direction of Southwestern Seminary and Southern Baptists in the 1920s? Scarborough helped to inaugurate a new era for Southern Baptists, and it is my hope that the following pages will make that clear.

Scarborough foresaw a new kind of denominationalism. His legacy is that of a more cooperative denomination — bringing all Southern Baptists together to focus on a common purpose. He directed a great deal of energy into molding a more wide-reaching denomination that embraced all facets of Christian ministry. Evangelism — winning converts to Christianity — always remained the central focus for Scarborough, and he urged Baptists to keep it as theirs as well.

However, the positive forces of evangelism and denominationalism were not the only things that attracted Scarborough's attention. There were problems to be dealt with as well. Southwestern Seminary seemed to always be home-base for such problems, and whether it was seeing the institution through the financial struggles of the Depression, or defending himself against the relentless attacks of fundamentalist leader J. Frank Norris, Scarborough was always up to the job.

In it all, Scarborough was a completely devoted Southern Baptist. His dream of a broader call to evangelism and a deeper commitment by churches and individuals was couched in the traditions and aspirations of Southern Baptists. His New Denominationalism was tailor-made by a lifelong Southern Baptist. In fact, it was a denominational design encompassing the whole of the Southern Baptist Convention.

Lee Rutland Scarborough is a major figure in Baptist history. As president of the great Southwestern Seminary and a leader of the Southern Baptist Convention, he proved to be an able administrator, fund-raiser, and evangelist. His management of the 75 Million Campaign gave new impetus to Southern Baptist outreach and identity. The Convention that he joined in the 1890s and the one he left behind in the 1940s was not the same. He had helped change it.

Understanding Scarborough is important in understanding Southern Baptists in this century. How would Southern Baptists have turned out differently if there had never been an L. R. Scarborough? Would they have had such a strong stand on cooperation? Maybe not. And would Southwestern Seminary have survived its many trials without the leadership of Scarborough? It's not likely. Wherever L. R. Scarborough went, he made a difference.

He spent his life "Calling Out the Called," and his legacy of evangelism and ministerial training continues among Southern Baptists. From the spoken to the written word, he placed divine calling and denominational zeal at the top of the Baptist "to do" list. For Scarborough, when all was said and done, calling and denomination became one and the same.

The intense denominational devotion expressed by Scarborough did not develop in a vacuum. Instead, the familial experience of a Baptist home and heritage caused him to choose a particular direction for his life and career. He was given a Baptist education by his parents and by academic institutions that together helped shape the ideology of a denominationalist.

Southern Baptists embraced a New Denominationalism in this century, and it was due in great part to the work of L. R. Scarborough. But, before that could happen, he had to first truly become a Baptist.

Acknowledgments

As always in a work of this size, there are many people to thank. H. Leon McBeth rekindled my interest in history several years ago and particularly awakened my interest in Church History. He has been and continues to be an inspiration and guide in historical study. And certainly historian W. R. Estep has had his own influence upon me.

My friend Alan Lefever cataloged the Scarborough Collection at Southwestern Seminary and was the first to mention that I might find L. R. Scarborough interesting. He was right. And then he so ably led the way in the series on Texas Baptists with his biography of Scarborough's mentor, B. H. Carroll.

Ed Eakin deserves a special thanks. He had the original vision for this series and was eager to include Scarborough.

And then there is my band of supporters: friends like Karen and John Bullock, Stephen Stookey, Mike Williams, James Wiles, Curt Horn, and Kevin Hall, to mention just a few. I have also received a great deal of encouragement from Chip Conyers, Gene Barber, and Scott Walker, who I am lucky enough to call friends.

I am especially thankful for my wife, Leslie, who is my partner in all things. She is a constant source of love and support.

The presence of Christ gives me hope for each day. I have sensed him on every page of this book and my faith has again been strengthened.

Lee Rutland Scarborough

CHAPTER 1

Becoming Baptist

The Bible and the Southern Baptist world-view were daily fare in the home of George W. Scarborough. A Baptist preacher, Scarborough led his family to reach out to the West Texas communities around them with the hope of the Gospel. His devout wife, Martha, joined wholeheartedly in fulfilling the Great Commission in their home and region. The Scarborough home was a place where there was always a warm welcome and a hot meal for anyone in need.

Lee Rutland Scarborough was one of several children that his mother was responsible for each day. Yet, somehow, she knew that Lee, the youngest son, was different. It was his destiny, she believed, to follow in his father's footsteps as a Baptist preacher. Martha Scarborough began praying for Lee to be called into the ministry when he was an infant and apparently never stopped.

George W. Scarborough and Martha Elizabeth Rutland had been married on June 20, 1850.[1] Martha was two or three years senior to George, but theirs was a seemingly happy and successful marriage.[2] There were nine children born to the Scarboroughs, only five of which survived to adulthood. Lee was the next to last child born and the youngest son.[3]

While July 4, 1870, may have seemed like any other Independence Day celebration for most people, it was a day of both joy and concern for George and Martha Scarborough. Their eighth child, Lee, had been born.[4] At the same time, however, the birth had taken a heavy toll on Martha, who would be bedridden for several weeks as a result of the trauma.

Although born in Colfax, Louisiana, Lee Scarborough would spend his formative years in West Texas. When Lee was about four years old, the family moved to a climate more suitable for his mother's frail health.[5] It was on a Texas ranch that young Scarborough came to know the meaning of family life.

FAMILY HERITAGE AND HOME LIFE

George W. Scarborough was born in 1831 somewhere in the state of Mississippi. He moved with his family to Louisiana as a young boy. It was there that he met and later married Martha Elizabeth Rutland. She, too, was an elective citizen of Louisiana, since she was born in Tennessee in or about 1828.[6] The two were married under the auspices of the state of Louisiana in 1850. George was nineteen years old and Martha was twenty-two.[7]

The Scarboroughs lived in East Texas for a few years in the 1850s, but eventually returned to Louisiana. During the Civil War, George Scarborough continued his bivocational life of preaching and seeking out other types of work to support his ever-growing family. There is a bill of record extant which shows that on October 10, 1863, George Scarborough, along with his brother-in-law W. R. Rutland, was employed by the Confederacy to transport "government stores."[8] Scarborough and Rutland moved supplies for the Confederate army by wagon and train. It was through this kind of contract labor that George Scarborough was able to provide for his family in somewhat uncertain times.

George and Martha Scarborough were the parents of nine children. Three girls and one of the boys died during or very near infancy.[9] The first child, Eugenia, came in March 1852, less than two years after the Scarboroughs' union. Children came in succession every two or three years until 1872, when Nancy was born. She was the last child and did not survive.[10]

Lee Rutland Scarborough was the next to last child, born in 1870. His mother was forty-two years old at his birth and almost died during the process of maternity and delivery.[11] This youngest son, called "Lee" by family and friends, was also given his mother's family name—Rutland. Even in this gesture Martha Scarborough somehow knew that this son was to be more special to her than the rest. Indeed, she endowed him with her emotional and spiritual support from the very first.[12]

Scarborough shared a touching story recounted to him by his mother in later years:

> The human beginning of the influence leading to my salvation was in the prayer of my mother in my behalf when I was an infant. She climbed out of bed, having gone down toward the grave that I might live, and crawled on her knees across the floor to my little cradle when I was three weeks of age, and prayed that God would save me in His good time and call me to preach.[13]

It was a calling that Scarborough would not yield to until he was into adulthood and living hundreds of miles from home. Yet, his mother could see from the beginning that this particular son was destined to a life of servanthood in the ministry.

Martha has been described as "a woman remarkable for gentleness, poise, courage, religious fervor and the spirit of uncomplaining sacrifice."[14] But she was also a fragile person, who may have endured a few too many pregnancies. Her frail health was the main reason that George Scarborough moved his family from Louisiana to West Texas when Lee was quite young.[15] Although a native of Louisiana, L. R. Scarborough would bear all the characteristics of an authentic Texan.

LIFE IN WEST TEXAS

While the Scarboroughs initially lived in McLennan County, it was in Jones County, at a place called Truby Mound, that the family finally settled.[16] The entire Scarborough clan made the move to Texas, including the two older sons with their wives and children. L. R. Scarborough could count himself among the charter residents of this West Texas region.[17]

The ranch became the center of life for the Scarboroughs. Cattle, cowmen, and round-ups were the common store of the West Texas atmosphere, and it was a lifestyle that L. R. Scarborough quickly came to love.[18] For his father, George, it was a dual existence of ranch and pulpit. The preaching of the Gospel message remained the focus of the elder Scarborough's life, and he came to be very adept with the brand of Christianity as well as the branding iron.

George W. Scarborough was a thoroughly dedicated Baptist preacher. He operated somewhat as an itinerant evangelist by sharing his witness in several towns within reasonable distance of the ranch. He not only filled the pulpits of already established churches, but had a hand in starting congregations in places like Abilene, Big Spring, and Anson.[19] A few years earlier, while residing in McLennan County, Scarborough had received ordination under the ministry of B. H. Carroll. He carried with him the same broad-based spirit of Carroll and eventually passed his admiration for the great preacher on to his youngest son, Lee.[20]

The Scarborough ranch in West Texas was an unaffected land of adventure — especially for a boy in his formative years. George could stand in the doorway of their log house and raise his rifle on every imaginable sort of wild game. Within only a few steps of the house there were deer, turkey, buffalo, and antelope just waiting to become the main course at the Scarborough supper table.[21] It was a table that was rarely without a visitor. Lee Scarborough remembered:

> I think probably for twelve or fifteen years there was scarcely a night or a meal that we did not have company. I have seen as many as twenty-five cowmen stay all night at our house the same night. Travelers would often stay for days with us. My father never charged a person for a meal or for lodging in our house in our lives. Great hospitality marked our home all the years of my memory. In those frontier days when there were but few people in the country, we welcomed visitors from anywhere and offered them the hospitality of a good home.[22]

The example of his father had a profound impact on Scarborough as he observed a man generous in both spiritual and material effects.

The "family altar" was also a regular feature of the Scarborough home.[23] This practice was carried on nightly just after clearing the table of the evening meal. Family and guests alike were invited to gather together for Scripture reading, a hymn or two, and a few moments of solemn prayer. It was in this way that George Scarborough was able to give to the cowmen visitors vivid evidence of life in a Christian home.

It was a mixed environment on the West Texas ranch: one of constant threat from the wild or from Indian raids, and one of serenity where a young boy could hear the whispered prayers of his father and mother. "Many a night," recalled Lee Scarborough, "while the Scripture reading, song, and prayer were in progress, I have heard the howl of the loper wolf and other wild animals just outside the door."[24]

PARENTAL INFLUENCE

When one considers the reasons behind L. R. Scarborough's decision to enter the ministry, it is the image of his parents which comes to the foreground as the primary factor in his ultimate determination. Scarborough himself said that the "one man who looms up most in those days of my struggle with the call to preach is my father."[25] It was not only the example which his father had laid before him all the years of his youth, but the direct assertions by his father that led to the final resolution. "My boy," Scarborough remembered his father saying, "God's plan is for you to preach."[26] The younger Scarborough could not erase the deep impact of his father's words.

Scarborough was forever proud to be the son of "one of the best men God ever made."[27] George Scarborough's physical size (he weighed more than 250 pounds) was matched by the size of his love for family and lost souls. He and Lee became good friends early on and remained so until his death in 1899.[28] George set the standard for his young son and proved himself to be an able worker for the advancement of God's Kingdom—particularly in the area of church planting. R. T. Hanks, a renowned Baptist preacher in nineteenth-century Texas, recalled George with fondness. "He always helped; I never knew him to hinder," Hanks said.[29] This was the kind of example that L. R. Scarborough would come to emulate.

Equally important to the development of Scarborough toward a career in the ministry was the influence of his mother. It was Martha Scarborough who first believed her son to be a chosen messenger of the Gospel.[30] It was Martha, too, who would be the impetus of Scarborough entering student life at Baylor University.[31]

In addition to risking her own health to utter a prayer of petition at the side of young Lee's crib, she also continued in her own way to encourage her son toward the pastorate. Scarborough cherished the memory of a singular afternoon when he was about ten:

> I was playing in the sand just under the window in our log house in Jones County, Texas. Mother, sitting at the window, called me to her. I can remember now across the years her sweet voice saying, "Son, I want to see you." I sat on a stool, on which she had been resting her feet, at her knee and listened to the story, the sweetest of all the ages, how Christ was born of the Virgin Mary, was baptized of John in the Jordan, lived, taught, healed, preached, . . . and was crucified on Calvary, buried in Joseph's tomb, and rose again for the salvation and justification of a lost world. Mother's voice was mellow and tender and her speech was interupted *[sic]* by tears and sobs as she told me that story. I pillowed my head on her loving lap and wept the first bitter tears of conviction.[32]

Although Scarborough did not express his faith at that moment, it was an event marked with real intensity on his consciousness.

One cannot underestimate the sway of Scarborough's parents in relation to his conversion and decision to enter the ministry. In strictly human terms, their example and witness was at the heart of Scarborough turning toward Christ. For the remainder of his life, L. R. Scarborough pointed to his parents as the ruling factor in the direction which his life and career followed. "I count as the richest inheritance of my life," he said, "that which my father and mother left me and the other children in faithful lives of consecration and service to God and humanity." [33]

The influence of George and Martha Scarborough did not stop at the point of decision for Christ. It was not just a Christian life which the couple had modeled for their youngest son. Instead, it was the Baptist way of life which the two for so many years had lived out for family and community to observe. When L. R. Scarborough yielded to the Holy Spirit and settled on the service of vocational ministry, there was no question about what

Becoming Baptist 7

kind of pulpit he would fill. There was never a moment of doubt as to which denomination Scarborough would serve. The Scarboroughs were Southern Baptists, and in their son Lee they had shaped a denominationalist. He was, to be sure, a decidedly *Baptist* denominationalist.

THE COWBOY YEARS

The West Texas life offered a great deal of adventure but little education. For the young Lee Scarborough, the most valuable instruction came on the back of various horses while working as a cowboy. While there was little time for formal education on the range, the Scarboroughs did manage to provide bits and pieces of training for their son. Standard instruction would have to wait for the staid academic halls of Baylor University. In the meantime, young Scarborough lived an escapade of a boy's dreams.

Scarborough experienced the kind of reality one would expect on a West Texas ranch in the 1880s. It was a life of horses, cattle, roping, and wearing a gun and holster as a regular part of dress.[34] He became expert not only in riding and roping but also in handling a six-shooter. He readily took on the whole persona of a nineteenth-century cowboy. Scarborough first climbed into a saddle at age eight and virtually lived there until he was sixteen.[35] It was the rough life of a cowboy, Scarborough believed, which invested in him the stamina and physical strength to withstand the hectic and often stressful years of his ministry.[36]

Indeed, it was not an easy or safe lifestyle. The times of cattle round-up were particularly dangerous. It was not a scene of neatly fenced ranches with each owner's cattle separated. Instead, it was open-range country with thousands of cattle intermingling and roaming free. Twice a year, during round-up, cowmen from all the surrounding ranches would join together and sort out the cows which belonged to individual owners. This was an arduous task.[37]

Scarborough was injured on several occasions. Apart from the everyday cuts and bruises which came from running cows through the jagged West Texas brush, there were also incidents where he was seriously wounded. In one year Scarborough broke his right leg three times — each time while on horseback.[38] On another day he fell off of a horse and incurred a concussion (or what Scarborough called "stunning my brain").[39] He was totally unconscious for twenty-four hours. Fortunately, however, Scarborough was an extremely healthy young man and soon recovered from these various injuries.

During round-up the cowmen slept in the open field. A pillow was a "luxury," Scarborough recalled, and most of the men simply used their saddles to rest their heads.[40] While a somewhat harsh existence, it was one where a boy could learn to ride a fast horse and rope a running steer. It was high adventure for Scarborough, and he became quite a competent roper — a skill he never lost and was able to use in later years to attract cowmen to revival meetings.[41]

The other cowboys nicknamed Scarborough "The Dogie" and on one occasion, with another boy called "The Kid," he roped a particularly ornery bull that needed to be de-horned.

> Just as I got ready to throw my rope over my shouldres *[sic]* and give it the cowboy turn for his forefeet, the bull wheeled and made for my horse. His keen bull-killing horns ran through the hair of the tail of my horse and he plunged at him. As he did it, I dropped my rope as a trap for his forefeet. He was going one way and I was going the other . . . and when we reached the other end of the rope, the bull changed ends, his feet went into the air, and he came down out of the air on his back with a thump.[42]

It was this kind of daring that earned young Scarborough the respect of his fellow ranch-hands. One must remember that at the time Lee was only fourteen or fifteen years old. He was quite a remarkable young man.

THE SCHOOL YEARS

In 1886, at age sixteen, Scarborough's cowboy life came to an end. His father moved the family into the town of Merkel, Texas, and Scarborough entered the school there.[43] He was innocent of much education until that time, but he would become just as proficient in the classroom as he had been on the range.

Because of his responsibilities on the ranch, Scarborough had spent only a small portion of any given year in school. His first experience in the classroom came in McLennan County at the Hog Creek Schoolhouse.[44] Scarborough later remembered nothing about that year except a speech he made one Friday afternoon: "My head is large, My breast is small; God bless the girls, I love them all."[45] He quipped that it was the only poetry he ever remembered.

The next encounter with academia came in Jones County, when the family hired a cousin, Emma Scarborough, to teach the children.[46] Her work began in the Scarborough's log house at Truby Mound, but soon a schoolhouse was built a few miles to the south at Clear Fork Creek.[47] Scarborough was a fast learner and once won a prize for being the first to recite the multiplication table. His only other elementary education was accomplished in Anson and Merkel.[48]

Scarborough's mother always intended for him to graduate from Baylor University. One Sunday when he was ten or eleven, an agent for Baylor spoke at his church. Scarborough was confused by the speech, but his mother tried to explain to him about Baylor on the ride home in the wagon. Scarborough was so dumbfounded at the time that he thought "Baylor University" was the name of some kind of wild animal.[49] Patiently his mother deciphered the agent's message, and Scarborough later rejoiced that in "that plastic moment God created in my little heart a quiet hunger for an education."[50]

Interestingly, a day in court forever changed the direction of Scarborough's life. When he was about sixteen, in 1886 or 1887, a trial was being held in Anson at the Jones County Courthouse. A man had been accused of murder, and Scarborough decided to take a day off from the ranch and witness the high drama in the courtroom. The cowboy who entered the court that day and the young man who left were quite different.[51]

The lawyer for the defense was Judge K. K. Leggett. His impassioned plea for the man's life greatly impressed Scarborough. "This great lawyer held me spellbound for an hour," Scarborough recalled.[52] Although Leggett's client was convicted, a West Texas cowboy was given a new vision for his life. He left the courthouse determined to obtain an education and "resolved to be somebody."[53] His ambition for a legal career had been born.[54]

With his new dream in mind, Scarborough entered Baylor University in 1888.[55] He counts his education up to that time to have been the sixth- or seventh-grade level.[56] It was not easy for Scarborough to leave his family, nor for his parents to let him go. The family altar on the evening before his departure was a somber time where little was said and few hymns were sung. But the Scarboroughs were settled on their youngest son entering Baylor University.[57]

Scarborough's mother, in particular, was resolved on sending Lee to college. After years of living in a log house and saving every extra penny to build a more suitable home, she gave up her dream of another house to pay for the Baylor tuition. The house fund was diverted into Scarborough's education and "the house," said Scarborough, "was never built."[58]

The Baylor experience was a time of real growth for Scarborough. He entered as a freshman in January of 1888 and immediately began demonstrating his gift for learning. His first report card, issued on March 25, 1888, showed Scarborough excelling in virtually every subject.[59] He also participated in extra-curricular activities, such as the Erisophian Literary Society.[60] After four years of study he received a bachelor of arts degree, in 1892.[61]

Perhaps equally important to the formal study at Baylor were the Sunday morning worship services at First Baptist Church in Waco. The morning that Scarborough left for Baylor his father had extracted a promise from him that may have had one of the most lasting influences on his life and education:

> I want you to promise me that every Sunday morning while you are in Baylor you will go to hear Dr. [B. H.] Carroll preach, and without taking any notes you will try to remember his sermon; and in the afternoon I want you to write me what he said, his text, the Scripture he read, the outline of his sermon, and all you can remember.[62]

Scarborough faithfully kept this pledge and soon became quite adroit in rewriting Carroll's sermons. Later, as president of Southwestern Seminary, Scarborough made a significant confession about the practice: "As I look back over it now I count that this was my theological education."[63] Baylor and Carroll had much to offer the young cowboy from West Texas.

The idea of a legal career had gripped Scarborough for

Above: *Scarborough (center) as Baylor student, c. 1890.*
Below: *Baylor graduating class, 1892.*

many years. As a result, in 1895 he moved to New Haven, Connecticut, and enrolled in Yale University to prepare for a life with the bar.[64] Amazingly, this young man from Texas, with an unorthodox elementary education, rose almost to the top of his class his first year at Yale. In a class of 277, he was one of thirteen students to be chosen for the prestigious Phi Beta Kappa award.[65] Scarborough spent two years at Yale and graduated in 1896 with his second bachelor of arts degree.[66]

While at Yale, however, Scarborough turned away from his aspiration of becoming an attorney. During his senior year he finally yielded to a long suppressed call to the ministry.[67] He returned to Texas and entered the pastorate at Cameron.

In 1899, after his first three years as a pastor, Scarborough once again left Texas to continue his education. This time, however, it was not a law degree he was pursuing, but theological training at the Southern Baptist Seminary in Louisville, Kentucky.[68] There he sat under Baptist giants like E. Y. Mullins, A. T. Robertson, W. O. Carver, and J. R. Sampey.[69]

Scarborough thoroughly enjoyed the study at Southern, but he was unable to remain for the full course. In 1900, just before the final exams of his first year at Southern, Scarborough was recalled to Texas. A brother, George Adolphus Scarborough, had been killed by train robbers.[70]

Scarborough never returned to Southern and thus could claim only one year of formal theological education. The man who would climb to the summit of Southern Baptist academic leadership would look not to the dignified halls of Southern Seminary but to the pulpit of B. H. Carroll as the foundation of his theology and ministry.

TRANSFORMATION AND DIVINE CALL

Although raised in a pious home, Scarborough did not become a Christian until he was seventeen years old. A few years earlier he had joined the Baptist church in Anson and had even been baptized. However, Scarborough was convinced that he was not at that time a Christian.[71] It was in 1887, while a Cumberland Presbyterian revival was being held in Merkel, that true conviction came upon Scarborough.

One evening, after attending a revival meeting, Lee was studying when his mother came into the room to once again bear witness for Christ. Scarborough, in the depths of conviction, lashed out at his mother and said, "I do not want to hear about your Savior."[72] The next day he left school early to go to the nearby church building for prayer. Scarborough later shared that on the way to the church in Merkel he accepted Christ.[73]

Scarborough discounted his first baptism as merely "immersion."[74] It was at the hands of B. H. Carroll in 1889 that Scarborough was immersed in what he considered his first real baptism.[75] So, at the age of nineteen, Scarborough became a full-fledged member of a Baptist church.

One could say that Scarborough's call to the ministry began when he was only three weeks old, the night that his mother crawled out of her sick bed to kneel beside his crib and pray for God to save her son and make him a preacher.[76] Practically speaking, however, Scarborough submitted to the divine call while a student at Yale University.

It was to his father, though, that Scarborough pointed as the most direct human element in his call. Just before Lee left for Yale in 1895, his father had confided: "My boy, God's plan is for you to preach."[77] Although bound for pre-law studies at Yale, Scarborough could not forget the words of his father. Within his first year in New Haven, he had turned away from the law and toward the ministry.

On April 16, 1896, in his dormitory room at Yale, Scarborough consented to enter the ministry.[78] Three days later he wrote a letter to his parents about his new decision. This important document, partially reproduced here, gives valuable insight into Scarborough's call.

> [A]fter a long and heart-tearing struggle of some months I have reached the conclusion that I *must enter and give my life to the ministry.* . . . I am perfectly conscious of the fact and thoroughly believe the truth, that the Holy Spirit has absolutely encased my heart, grasped my very soul and compelled it by a persuasion not of my own to give up all, . . . to the work of preaching and teaching and living the Gospel of Christ. I have successfully resisted the desires and pleadings of my kinfolks and my friends, I have successfully proved my inability, my incapacity to do the work of a preacher; I have overcome and

vanquished all prudential matters and excuses but the stirring within my deepest soul, the divine compulsion of power within I could not overcome nor throw off, so I have with a joy as boundless as the heart can contain, humbly submitted and have not a shadow of a doubt about the source of my call nor a regret in any shape whatsoever that I have submitted.... I feel *utterly helpless* in myself, without a knowledge of the merest beginning of the duties and preparation of a preacher, incapacitated completely, yet with Isaiah I can say "The Lord also is wise," and I trust Him for the direction of the current of this feeble life of mine. My whole being is turned "right about," everything is revolutionized. I must begin life again and from a new base of operations. I did not want to preach, the Lord knows I did not. I exerted my fullest strength to get out of it but I simply *could not*, that is all, and retain any hope of happiness or peace in life.[79]

There was a good deal of celebration at the Scarborough home in Texas when the letter arrived. Scarborough's father wrote him within a week and declared that his prayers had been answered.[80] The elder Scarborough now encouraged his son to begin preaching immediately.

Scarborough finished his degree at Yale in 1896. He returned to Texas and preached his first sermon at First Baptist Church in Abilene on June 26.[81] It was the first of many sermons to come. Scarborough was now wholly aimed at the pastorate.

PASTORAL EXPERIENCE

In August 1896, Scarborough was serving in his first pastorate. He accepted the call from the Baptist church in Cameron, Texas. In a few years he would return to the pulpit of his first sermon as pastor. Thus, Scarborough's pastoral years would be spent in only two churches over a period of twelve years.[82]

The Cameron church initially paid Scarborough $50 per month and provided a parsonage. The salary was raised each year to a peak of $100 per month. Scarborough invited his parents to live with him in Cameron, and they both remained with him for the rest of their lives.[83]

The most remarkable part of the Cameron ministry was the great increase in membership. When Scarborough accepted the

First Baptist Church of Cameron, Texas.

position in 1896, there were approximately 200 members. By the time he accepted the call to Abilene in 1901, Scarborough had increased the Cameron church to almost 500 members.[84] One might say he had the "Midas Touch" for growth. It was a trait he would prove in both pastorates and as president of Southwestern Seminary.

Perhaps the most important event of the Cameron years was Scarborough's engagement and marriage to Mary P. (Neppie) Warren of Abilene.[85] Careful not to show undue attention to any of the young ladies in Cameron, Scarborough's interest was aroused when friends told him of young Miss Warren. Although she was engaged to another man at the beginning of their acquaintance, the engagement between Scarborough and Warren was not long in coming.[86] They were married on February 4, 1900.[87]

Since the wedding took place in the middle of Scarborough's year at Southern Seminary, the couple returned to Louisville together to complete his term there. Mrs. Scarborough even joined in Seminary studies, although not enrolled.[88] In a few months the Scarboroughs were back in Cameron to resume the duties of the pastorate.

Scarborough dearly loved his wife and believed her to be the perfect mate for a pastor.[89] In March 1901 their first child, George Warren, was born. Five other children would follow.[90] From all evidence, Lee and Neppie Scarborough were happy and devoted partners in marriage and ministry.[91]

Scarborough with wife and first child.

The Cameron church was satisfied with their pastor and his new wife. However, another church with a more challenging ministry was also interested in the Scarboroughs. The move to Abilene came in 1901.

Scarborough became pastor of First Baptist Church, Abilene, in August 1901.[92] He accepted the position at his Cameron salary of $100 per month. On his first anniversary in August 1902, however, remuneration was increased by $25 per month.[93] By 1908 the Abilene salary was $2,500 annually.[94]

The growth experienced at the Cameron church was duplicated in Abilene. In addition to increasing membership threefold from 400 to well over 1,000, Scarborough led in establishing

Becoming Baptist

Above: *Scarborough's first home in Abilene, Texas.*
Below: *Scarborough's second home in Abilene.*

two mission churches of First Baptist. By 1908 both were independent churches in their own right.[95]

Scarborough's first efforts on the denominational level also came during the Abilene pastorate. H. E. Dana pointed out that Scarborough's "policy as a pastor [was] to press the great missionary and denominational causes."[96] It was this policy which led him to become involved in raising funds for Simmons College (now Hardin-Simmons University). This was, said Dana, Scarborough's "first conspicuous denominational service."[97]

Although Simmons College had opened for classes in 1892, it remained somewhat unsteady financially through the rest of the nineteenth century. In the end, it was Scarborough, as pastor of First Baptist, Abilene, who led in stabilizing the city's Baptist college.[98] A Simmons College committee had been formed in the church as soon as August 1902, if not earlier.[99] While the committee concentrated on improving the buildings and property of the institution,[100] Scarborough focused on securing a new president for the college.[101]

In the Simmons College affair one sees for the first time Scarborough's flair at fund-raising that would become one of his calling cards in years to come. When he learned that Dr. O. H. Cooper, president of Baylor University, might be interested in moving to Simmons, Scarborough sprang into action.[102] The one obstacle to the move was the financial condition at Simmons. Scarborough proposed a plan to the board of trustees for a guarantee to Cooper of $2,000 per year above operating expenses. The guarantee was to be in effect for five years.[103] The trustees balked at the idea. Scarborough then took his proposal to area businessmen and in less than two days had obtained the five-year guarantee.[104] Cooper changed presidencies and joined Scarborough in Abilene to lay a firm foundation for Simmons College.

First Baptist Church fully supported Scarborough in his labor for Simmons. In his remaining years in Abilene, he helped raise money for two new buildings at the college—Anna and Cowden Halls.[105] One year Scarborough traveled for a total of eight months representing the college, but the church did not complain and continued to pay his full salary.[106]

While in Abilene, Scarborough began displaying his colors as a denominationalist. He loved the pastorate and even considered it the "preacher's throne,"[107] but it became more and more

Becoming Baptist 19

Left top: *Scarborough as chaplain of Abilene Fire Department.*

Bottom: *Scarborough in his study in Abilene.*

obvious that he was called to a broader ministry. In 1908, after twelve years as a pastor, Scarborough again yielded to the divine voice and agreed to leave Abilene. Only this time the voice was not conveyed by his father, but by the deep intonations of B. H. Carroll.

SUMMARY

Lee Rutland Scarborough was raised in a decidedly Southern Baptist family. His father, George, was a Baptist preacher, who served as a kind of bivocational itinerant evangelist. His mother, Martha, by choice a Baptist, was a deeply devoted woman who prayed for her son and lived out a consistent Christian witness. It was no accident that L. R. Scarborough graduated from a Southern Baptist college, attended a Southern Baptist seminary, and became a Southern Baptist pastor. From the beginning he was shaped into a denominationalist.

The molding of Scarborough continued under the ministry of B. H. Carroll. It was not the Southern Baptist Theological Seminary in Louisville that grounded Scarborough in Baptist theology. Instead, his theology took shape as a result of Carroll's preaching at First Baptist Church in Waco. When Scarborough looked for the human element in his call to ministry, he focused on the influence of his father. However, when he considered the foundation of his Baptist theology, he gave preeminence to B. H. Carroll.

Scarborough's experience as pastor of First Church, Abilene, cemented his denominational ideology. It was his "policy" to place the concerns of the denomination at the forefront of his ministry.[108] His work on behalf of Simmons College identified him with the larger causes of Southern Baptists. By 1908 he was no longer just the pastor of a Texas Baptist church. Scarborough had become the spokesperson for all West Texas Baptists as he traveled the state pushing the importance of Simmons College. He arrived at Abilene as a Southern Baptist pastor and departed as a Southern Baptist leader.

It may be impossible to pinpoint the exact date that Scarborough became a full-fledged denominationalist. He had grown up in a home steeped in Baptist doctrine and followed his father into a Baptist pulpit. One can surmise, though, that his work in Abilene launched him into the role of denominational envoy. It was his promotion of an academic institution that brought attention to his talent and devotion. It was the call of another academic institution that sealed his legacy as a denominationalist.

CHAPTER 2

Building a Seminary

L. R. Scarborough served as the second president of Southwestern Baptist Theological Seminary, from 1915 until 1942. Prior to becoming president, however, Scarborough was a member of Southwestern's faculty as professor of evangelism. Indeed, he was on the charter faculty and continued to hold his professorship contemporaneously with the office of president until his retirement.

Seminary Hill, a few miles south of downtown Fort Worth, was the center of Scarborough's activity for most of his ministry. He spent more than thirty years at Southwestern and was closely identified with the Seminary and its mission. Although Southwestern began as the dream of B. H. Carroll, it was Scarborough who insured that the Seminary remained a reality. In a presidency that lasted four times longer than Carroll's, he led Southwestern through both good times and bad—including the years of the Great Depression.

Equally important to his service as president was his position on the faculty as professor of evangelism. B. H. Carroll created the world's first chair of evangelism (what he called the "Chair of Fire") and appointed Scarborough as its first occupant. Scarborough was comfortable with his identity as preacher/evangelist, and even as president of the Seminary he still considered his classes in evangelism a priority.

Scarborough's vision early in his presidency was to make an intimate connection between the Seminary and the Southern Baptist Convention. Originally chartered under the Baptist General Convention of Texas, Southwestern became an institution for all Southern Baptists during Scarborough's tenure. The denominational ideology that characterized his personal life came to typify the Seminary as well.

Not everyone shared Scarborough's loyalty to the denomination, however, and he was forced during his term as president to answer the charges of nay-sayers. In particular, Fort Worth pastor J. Frank Norris worked against Scarborough in both the personal and professional realms. While the dispute with Norris did not define the Scarborough presidency, it was a sad sequence of events which distracted Scarborough from more important matters.

In the end, Scarborough could look back on a successful ministry at Southwestern. The Seminary allowed him to stretch his talents for administration and fund-raising. It gave him a forum to share his views on evangelism. Perhaps most significantly, the building of Southwestern Seminary helped Scarborough express his Southern Baptist denominationalism in an enduring form.

B. H. CARROLL'S DREAM

Benajah Harvey Carroll (1843–1914) was the founder and first president of Southwestern Baptist Theological Seminary.[1] At least by 1905, Carroll believed that God was urging him to begin a seminary in Texas. He personally obtained promises from a number of Texas Baptists to help finance a theological institution. Approximately $32,000 was committed to undergird the first few years of operation.[2]

The Seminary grew out of the theological department of Baylor University in Waco, where Carroll was pastor of the First Baptist Church. He was on good terms with Oscar H. Cooper, president of Baylor from 1899 until 1902.[3] It was during Cooper's tenure that Carroll instituted Baylor's theological department.

The most popular photograph of B. H. Carroll.
— Courtesy Southwestern Baptist Theological Seminary Archives

By 1902, however, with the election of S. P. Brooks to Baylor's presidency, some tension developed over Carroll's involvement at the university. On one hand, Carroll was a teacher in the theological department; on the other, he was the president of the board of trustees. Robert A. Baker reported that Brooks "was not pleased with the unique administrative structure" that Baylor and Carroll had formed.[4] It was a strained relationship that was unable to last for long. In 1905 Carroll separated the theological department from the university, and what would become Southwestern Seminary opened in Waco as the Baylor Theological Seminary.

The name of the institution officially became Southwestern Baptist Theological Seminary in 1908.[5] The state of Texas issued the charter in March of that year.[6] J. B. Gambrell was named as president of the board of trustees, and at the May 1908 meeting of the board B. H. Carroll was formally elected president of the Seminary.[7] At the same meeting the charter faculty, consisting of six persons, was appointed. B. H. Carroll was considered a member of the faculty; A. H. Newman was named professor of Church History; Calvin Goodspeed was the appointee for systematic theology; Charles B. Williams was professor of New Testament Greek; Jeff D. Ray headed the homiletics section; and L. R. Scarborough was given the professorship in evangelism.[8]

THE CHAIR OF FIRE

B. H. Carroll established the world's first Chair in evangelism — a position he called the "Chair of Fire."[9] As early as 1906, Carroll was urging Scarborough to accept a place on his theological faculty. Besides getting him to take on teaching responsibilities, Carroll hoped to persuade Scarborough to represent the Seminary as field secretary (i.e., a fund-raising and recruiting agent). In Carroll's mind the two positions went together. Still, it was the evangelism Chair that most interested him. He wrote to Scarborough:

> There are perhaps many men who could do fairly well as field secretary. There are, *known to me now*, only two living men to whom I would offer *the Chair of Evangelism*. You are first. The other I suppose is absolutely inaccessible. I will try him if you decline. Failing both of you, I will take the case to Him who is never straightened for means and ask Him to fill this *Chair of Fire*.[10]

The decision to leave the pastorate of First Baptist, Abilene, and join the Seminary faculty was not easy for Scarborough. From 1906 onward Carroll constantly asked for Scarborough's answer. On January 11, 1908, Carroll wrote Scarborough two separate letters.[11] One focused on the professorship in evangelism and the other centered on the office of field secretary. While the second letter dealt with somewhat mundane matters concerning the duties of Seminary representative (such as securing support from churches), the first showed the persuasive powers of B. H. Carroll.

After promising Scarborough that Southwestern's evangelism professor would become "really famous,"[12] Carroll went on to recount some of Scarborough's attributes and to prick his curiosity about his professional potential.

> You have the religion, the fire, the afflatus, the conviction, the didactic capacity, but so far in your life-work you have dealt

mainly with *awakening* work rather than the careful, constructive and instructive. You need to enlarge your general range of investigation and to discipline your mind to great excellency of power on special lines.[13]

Carroll continued in his emotional appeal and laid out the "special lines" that he saw in Scarborough's future.

> My own heart is deeply concerned for this enterprise. The *need* of it is very great, and ever increases. But I am admonished that my time is short and oh I long to see the enterprise on deep-rooted, solid foundztions *[sic]* before I die. And I need to stand by me through thick and thin young men of hope, love, daring, and unflinching faith. Young men who believe in it, who have the spirit and devotion of sacrifice for it, and who without *shadow of doubt* will consecrate themselves on its altar, looking to the Master for approbation and reward. . . .
>
> I therrfore *[sic]*, loving you znd *[sic]* trusting you, and having with strong conviction looked to you from the beginning as a partner in this enterprise, now once more invite you to fall into line as a permanent working force, wholly and irrevocably committed to it.[14]

Considering the great admiration that Scarborough held for B. H. Carroll—and the obvious pressure administered—one can clearly understand H. E. Dana's words that the "proposition somehow very deeply gripped [Scarborough's] conscience."[15] Finally, in February 1908, while conducting a revival at First Baptist Church of Pine Bluff, Arkansas, Scarborough yielded to what he believed was a divine call to the Seminary.[16]

Charter faculty member Jeff D. Ray believed that Scarborough personified the "Chair of Fire." He looked to Scarborough as the chief cause of Southwestern's "reputation for evangelistic fervor."[17] Perhaps this was because Carroll and Scarborough agreed that the purpose of the Chair was "to keep the fires of Evangelism burning in all the hearts connected with the Seminary."[18]

The Seminary needed a permanent home where suitable buildings could be constructed and plans for a world-class institution could be carried out. Carroll immediately turned to L. R. Scarborough to lead in the relocation of Southwestern. It was a natural move for Carroll, because he had been looking to Scarborough for a number of years as his second-in-command.

MOVE TO FORT WORTH

It seemed obvious from the very beginning that Southwestern would need room in which to grow. Carroll looked northward to the Dallas/Fort Worth area for a permanent site for the Seminary campus.[19] While he remained in Waco, Carroll gave Scarborough the main responsibility of investigating various locations that might be appropriate for a large institution. It was a matter of accepted fact between the two men that they were building a first-class seminary.[20]

The faculty and Carroll himself hoped to place the Seminary in Dallas.[21] Perhaps the presence of First Baptist Church of Dallas and the Buckner Orphanage tended to make it look like more of an institutional city.[22] There was a debt problem among the Baptists of Dallas, however, with First Church, Gaston Avenue Church, and the Buckner Home in the process of meeting their own financial obligations.[23] Scarborough was concerned that Dallas was unable to offer the Seminary the proper facilities:

> I remember that I asked Dr. Carroll the following questions: . . . "What is the value of the First Baptist Church building?" He answered "More than $100,000."
> "What is the value of the Gaston Avenue Church building?" He answered "More than $100,000."
> I asked "What is the value of the Buckner Orphans' Home?" He said "Several hundred thousand dollars."
> "Now," I said, "what is the value of the building that is offered to us?" He said, "Probably $25,000." "Then," I said, "compared to these other institutions, doesn't it look as if the Southwestern Seminary in such a poor equipment would look like six bits?"[24]

Scarborough never knew whether his questions were the primary cause of the offer from Dallas being rejected, but he does admit that everyone's attention "immediately turned to Fort Worth."[25]

Carroll wanted to make certain that the churches of Fort Worth were serious in their commitment to the Seminary. He decided that the city should raise $100,000 as evidence of their dedication to building the institution and its facilities.[26] In September 1909 a meeting was held at the First Baptist Church of Fort Worth, where Carroll laid out his proposal for the Seminary.

Scarborough believed that those "who heard Dr. Carroll that night will probably never forget it. He was at his best."[27] The promise was made by Fort Worth leaders for the prescribed sum of money.

At the end of the meeting, Carroll announced that he would leave Scarborough in Fort Worth to explore the sites and make preparations for the coming of the Seminary.[28] Scarborough was shocked at this declaration. It was the first he had heard of Carroll's intention. He recalled:

> I had not the slightest idea up until the time of the closing words of Dr. Carroll's address before that crowd that he expected me to lead in the campaign in Fort Worth. It was the first big Seminary load that he put on me. I went back to my room at the hotel with my heart weighing a hundred tons. I think I prayed most of the night. Before day, greatly wearied and unspeakably burdened, a number of the great promises of God's word came to my heart, and while kneeling by the bedside God gave me the assurance that He would go with me and give me success, and one of the happiest moments of my life resulted.[29]

The invaluable experience of fund-raising and organization at Simmons College now came into full use for Scarborough. He later reported that the $100,000 was obtained "without serious difficulty."[30]

LOCATION AND BUILDING

On November 2, 1909, Scarborough reported to Southwestern's board of trustees on the progress being made in Fort Worth. He was able to convey that the entire amount of money had been secured and several sites were available. The board empowered Scarborough to procure property deeds and acquire the best locale.[31] The following week Scarborough was appointed to head a building committee.[32]

The site chosen was south of Fort Worth at the highest point of elevation in the area (thus, "Seminary Hill"). The vicinity of the campus was about thirty acres and the surrounding land covered almost 300 acres.[33] Scarborough felt that the location was perfect for the Seminary and was enhanced because it would be the sole Baptist institution in Fort Worth.[34]

In January 1910 the board of trustees approved the expense of renting an office for Scarborough in Fort Worth.[35] He stationed himself downtown in the Touraine Building.[36] The board also allowed Scarborough to hire a stenographer and allocated money to keep his car repaired.

Front view of construction of Fort Worth Hall in 1909.
— Courtesy Southwestern Baptist Theological Seminary Archives

Progress on obtaining cash-in-hand and engaging building contractors came quickly in the first few months of 1910. By February, Scarborough had banked $75,000 and was expecting the rest of the money in a matter of days.[37] In March a contract was signed to build Fort Worth Hall for $105,000.[38] The building, which housed offices, class and library space, and dormitory rooms, was ready for occupation by October 1910.

SPRING BIBLE CONFERENCE

Financial matters were not the only concern of Scarborough in 1910. He was also vitally interested in the kinds of instruction the Seminary would offer when it opened for classes in the coming academic year. While pastor of First Baptist, Abilene, Scarborough had participated in annual Spring Bible Conferences. He hoped to see Southwestern present the same sort of opportunity for the students.[39]

Scarborough laid out a rather extensive program of study. Within a span of ten days he planned to offer sixty-five lectures from Southern Baptist leaders like E. Y. Mullins, J. M. Frost, W. B. Riley, and, of course, Carroll himself.[40] He admitted that the lecture schedule was a bit weighty, but believed that such an extensive program would attract people from all across the country. Ever the promoter, he saw not only an opportunity to train students but to advance the cause of Southwestern Seminary.

The conference was held in the spring term of 1911. Although Scarborough hoped to make the ten-day conference a regular part of the Seminary program, it did not survive for many years.[41] Still, Scarborough believed the spring meeting had the power to "spread a mighty spiritual conflagration of holy evangelistic fire."[42] For Scarborough, at least, the fire kept burning.

Faculty of Southwestern in 1912.
– Courtesy Southwestern Baptist Theological Seminary Archives

FROM PROFESSOR TO PRESIDENT

Scarborough joined the charter faculty of Southwestern in 1908 as professor of evangelism. In addition to his teaching responsibilities were added the duties of agent and head of the building committee. He realized from the first that Carroll held a fatherly affection for him and expected a higher level of commitment from him.[43] What he did not know, however, was how soon he would be acting in behalf of his mentor. Indeed, Scarborough would in a short time become the president himself and mold the Seminary into his unique expression of denominationalism.

By 1912, B. H. Carroll could no longer handle the day-to-day operations of the Seminary. A. H. Newman, as dean of the faculty, attempted to compensate for Carroll's inability to meet his classes in English Bible by substituting other courses in the degree plan. This strategy worked throughout 1912. Then, in the early months of 1913, Carroll's condition deteriorated and he lapsed into a coma. His death appeared imminent; however, in May 1913, Carroll revived. When he learned of the extent of the changes made by Newman and the faculty, he called Newman and J. J. Reeve to his home and asked for their resignations.[44]

The experience made a deep impression on Carroll. He realized that he was too ill to cope with the duties of president. As usual, his thoughts turned to his "boy"—Lee Scarborough.[45]

Carroll wrote a letter to the board of trustees, which was read at the meeting on May 29, 1913. While Carroll lived for another eighteen months, the letter in effect passed the mantle to Scarborough.

> I hereby request that you designate some suitable person as assistant to the President of the Faculty—to hold such position for the ensuing year, or until such time as my health and strength may admit of my doing all the work which belongs to the office of President. And that the duties of such assistant be to aid the President in the details of his work and in the name of the President, do all such work and perform all such acts incident to, or falling within the scope of the duties or [sic] the President as the President may by general or specific request, direct such assistant to do and perform; and also in the absence or inability of the President, to do and perform all such work and duties as may be necessary to be done to keep the work of the President fully up to date, and that the said assistant be

invested with full authority to issue all vouchers, checks, receipts, etc. as may be necessary under the conditions existing at the time. . . .

And in view of his thorough understanding of the work and duties of the President, and his intimate acquaintance with the details of the work of the President as said work has heretofore been done, and his familiarity with the books and records kept by the President, I recommend that you name L. R. Scarborough as such assistant to the President.[46]

Scarborough had been given "full authority" by Carroll himself, and he was automatically accepted by the board. Beginning in 1913, then, Scarborough was — in practical terms — the president of Southwestern Seminary.

By the latter part of 1913, Carroll had fully accepted his terminal condition. In a private meeting with Scarborough he released any remaining vestige of his office. "I am going to have to turn it over to you," he told Scarborough.[47] Carroll was convinced that the burden of the Seminary had caused his illness, and he lamented to Scarborough: "I am sure it will kill you."[48]

Scarborough was now the official spokesperson for Southwestern. In November 1913 he gave the Seminary's annual report at the Texas Baptist Convention. Although still only "assistant to the president," he sounded like the heir-apparent that he was:

> Brethren of the Convention, let's build on Seminary Hill a Theological power house on the rocks of predestination, around the person of our Risen Redeemer, knowing no orders but His command, fearing nothing but His disfavor, loyal to His revealed will, carrying His Gospel of redeeming love and blood around the world in the holy fires of His Divine Spirit, till Jesus comes again.[49]

While he was still officially Carroll's assistant, the board recognized Scarborough's standing among the Seminary community. In May 1914 the assistant's salary was raised to $3,000 annually — equal to that of the president.[50] When Carroll died in November 1914, Scarborough was named "acting president" of the Seminary.[51]

Building a Seminary

SCARBOROUGH'S INAUGURATION

On February 9, 1915, L. R. Scarborough was unanimously elected as the second president of Southwestern Seminary. His salary was set at $4,000 per year.[52] By April 8 arrangements had been made for the official installation of the new president.[53] Programs were scheduled for morning, afternoon, and evening. Addresses at each session were made by fellow academic presidents like S. P. Brooks of Baylor University and E. Y. Mullins of Southern Seminary.[54] The final discourse of the evening was offered by Scarborough himself.

Scarborough's lecture was titled "The Primal Test of Theological Education" and centered on the characteristics and purpose of the Seminary.[55] After recounting a brief history of Southwestern, he turned to his two main points: what he called "fundamentals" and the "marks of an efficient ministry." Interestingly, Scarborough's denominationalism is a key feature of his manuscript.

In the new president's estimation the very first fundamental of Southwestern was its "Denominational Anchorage."[56] There was no question that on Seminary Hill one would find a "distinctively Baptist" institution.[57] Scarborough gave Carroll credit for anchoring Southwestern firmly to Baptist standards and for placing three "guards" against any movement away from the Baptist fold.

First, no professor was accepted on the Seminary faculty who was not a member of a "Missionary Baptist Church."[58] Second, each professor was required to subscribe to the New Hampshire Confession (a nineteenth-century confession of faith that was standard for Baptists at the time). The third guard set in place by Carroll was the assurance that all trustees were Baptists. Scarborough pledged to his listeners that Southwestern would "remain true to the doctrines of its founders and supporters."[59]

Scarborough sensed the need for a further word about the denominational loyalty of the Seminary. As one of his five "marks of an efficient ministry" he pointed to the essential of "Denominational Sympathy and Co-Operation":

> All seminaries that are worth while in producing an efficient ministry are in easy reach of the currents of the denominational life supporting them. These seminaries should feel

their accountability to and responsibility for such denominational life. Their professors and presidents and students should be in the heart of all kingdom activities, co-operant and vital. No seminary teacher has a moral right to poison the life of his denomination by erroneous and heretical teaching while he holds position and draws salary from such denomination. . . .

The seminary graduate should be a mighty co-operant force with all the denominational and kingdom agencies and institutions. He should be a builder, a constructive force. It is not enough that he should be known by his scholarly attainments, his grace and accuracy of speech, his eloquent appeals. He must do things, be a doer of the word.[60]

As the Seminary's new president, Scarborough reaffirmed the denominational ties to Southern Baptists. While Southwestern was still owned by the Baptist General Convention of Texas in 1915, Scarborough was already moving steadily to insure the connection of the Seminary to the Convention as a whole.

TRANSFER OF OWNERSHIP

From the first, Southwestern had been owned by Texas Baptists. Before 1920, however, ten state conventions—in the form of appointed trustees—had joined in the operation of the Seminary.[61] Scarborough believed that the ownership of the institution should reflect the involvement of a larger body of Southern Baptists than those within the borders of Texas. Within the first three years of his presidency, he was contemplating a change in ownership.

Scarborough's first move was to approach the faculty with his idea. The entire group supported the transfer.[62] Next, he went to the board of trustees, who in 1918 commissioned the president to inquire into the possibility of deeding the Seminary to the Southern Baptist Convention.[63] In April 1920 the board gave more power to Scarborough to actively pursue the matter.[64]

The transfer process took a total of seven years from inception to completion. In May 1923, at the Southern Baptist Convention in Kansas City, the board of trustees formally offered the Seminary to the messengers.[65] The matter was referred back to the Texas Convention for its annual meeting in November 1923, and a resolution was adopted in support of the transfer.[66]

On May 14, 1924, the board of trustees selected a committee to work with the Convention to organize the transfer.[67] By the time the Southern Baptist Convention met in Memphis in May 1925, Scarborough was able to report that all legal matters had been settled and the transfer of ownership was complete.[68] Scarborough's hope of effecting a closer connection between Southwestern and the denomination had become a reality.

Scarborough believed that the Seminary could help unify the denomination and further the mission of Southern Baptists. He also saw in the transfer of ownership a chance to link Seminary Hill to each church in the Convention. In 1925 he championed his cause:

> It [Southwestern] can furnish such denominational atmosphere, spirit and loyalty as that the leadership it trains will be in profound sympathy and full co-operation with all the missionary, educational and benevolent program of Southern Baptists. It proposes to give, as far as it can, a trained leadership to our churches which is thoroughly loyal and co-operant with all the work of our ongoing, progressive, militant churches.[69]

The denominationalism one would encounter at Southwestern, Scarborough felt, was unequaled at any other institution. The Seminary was able to "give soul-winners to every line and phase of the denominational task."[70] It was a denominationalism that flowed out of the president's commitment to Southern Baptists and merged the life of the Seminary with that of the entire Convention.

FINANCIAL MATTERS

L. R. Scarborough first began his financial involvement at Southwestern when the Seminary moved to Fort Worth. When B. H. Carroll decided that $100,000 would have to be raised by churches in the Tarrant Baptist Association before the institution would relocate in Fort Worth, it was Scarborough that he left behind to gather pledges.[71] From the very beginning, a primary function for Scarborough was fund-raising and money management.

Even though the pledge goal was met by Fort Worth Baptists, Scarborough and other Seminary leaders realized that more money was necessary to sustain and develop the institution. In 1913 he told Texas Baptists that fund-raising for the Seminary had been very successful. In only five years Southwestern's endowment had grown to $400,000, with an additional half-million dollars in land and buildings.[72] Still, Scarborough insisted that an additional $300,000 in endowment was needed. He called on the Baptists of Texas to make Southwestern's endowment a total of $700,000. "If you will give us this," he said, "we will do our best to *start* you a great seminary."[73]

As the world moved into war in the following years, however, the Seminary's endowment hovered at the $400,000 level.[74] Year after year—into the 1920s and 1930s—there was a pattern of deficit spending. For the decade 1926 through 1936, for example, there was a total deficit of almost $200,000. Each year the Seminary was underfinanced by almost $17,000 — quite a lot of money in the middle of the Depression.[75]

In addition, Southwestern was operating under a rather heavy debt. Fort Worth Hall had cost more to build than was originally expected, and land purchases had pushed the Seminary even further into negative spending.[76] By 1918 the Baptist

Aerial view of Southwestern Seminary, c. 1930.

General Convention of Texas had decided to attempt to better the Seminary's financial condition. Scarborough was named to head a committee to research the debt in all Texas Baptist schools. The committee made recommendations which included the issuance of bonds. As a result, the Texas Convention assumed Southwestern's indebtedness and in 1919 sold "Loyalty Bonds" to recoup its investment.[77]

Naturally, the Great Depression was a real hindrance to Southwestern's financial stability. Although 894 students were enrolled in May 1930, Scarborough was forced to cut faculty salaries and some positions because of the economy.[78] Less than one year later, conditions were so poor that the president asked the board to pay each faculty member at least one-half of his salary.[79] By May 1931 the Seminary's debt, mainly due to building projects, had risen to $459,000.[80] By 1932 the Depression had not only driven the debt up to almost the half-million mark but had taken its toll in the student body, with enrollment down to 587.[81]

Scarborough also incurred personal debt in relation to the Seminary. As early as 1923 he was borrowing up to $20,000 per year to help defray students' expenses.[82] Since Southwestern was unable to offer student loans, the president took personal charge of individuals in financial straits. It was not a practice that he wished to continue on a permanent basis, but Scarborough insured that untold numbers of students completed their degrees.

He was not, however, above reminding students of their obligations to the Seminary. In the mid-1920s he began a custom of extracting promises from students to donate $10 per year until age sixty-five. By 1928 more than 300 students had made such a pledge, but many had not kept current in their payments. In a letter to these alumni Scarborough wrote: "I do not think it is for lack of love for the dear old Seminary nor a lapse in conscience in meeting a sacred pledge."[83] He proposed that for each person who paid his or her $10 pledge for the 1927-28 academic year he would forgive any remaining balance. Finally, loyalty to Southwestern was more important to Scarborough than $10.

Another way in which Scarborough invested personal funds in the Seminary was through "The Seminary Hill Street Railway Company." The existing municipal streetcar line ended more than one mile from the campus. Anyone who wished to go into the city had to make his way over an open field.[84] In 1911 the board of trustees gave the streetcar project to Scarborough and asked him to invest $8,000 of his own money.[85] As security for his investment, the trustees gave Scarborough ten acres of property adjacent to Southwestern. Scarborough, along with partners J. K. Winston and H. C. McCart, chartered the company in 1912 and ran the private line (although somewhat ineffectively) for two years. In 1914 the city car took over the route.[86]

In 1925, the same year the Seminary's ownership was transferred to the Southern Baptist Convention, the widow of Texas Baptist George E. Cowden donated $150,000 to Southwestern. There was a need for another building, and Mrs. Cowden's gift was for the construction of a School of Gospel Music. Scarborough had worked with George Cowden when raising money for Simmons College and the two had become fast friends. Mrs. Cowden explained that it was because of her husband's confidence in Scarborough that she wished for him to personally oversee the construction of "Cowden Hall."[87]

Robert A. Baker revealed that while the building was needed, Scarborough realized that the amount donated by the Cowden estate would not be sufficient to finish the project.[88] Hence, the Seminary went further into debt.

Cowden Hall, Southwestern, under construction.

Building a Seminary 39

One way that Scarborough provided operating capital for the Seminary during these lean years was through citrus fruit orchards he obtained through donations and by trading property. In 1928, 200 acres in the lower Rio Grande Valley were given by Mrs. Flora Mills Carter for the purpose of growing fruit and using the profit from sales for the Seminary.[89] A second tract of 1,000 acres was acquired by trading business property in Dallas for the land. In the mid-1920s, G. W. Bottoms had given the Dallas property to Southwestern and the Buckner Orphanage to share equally.[90] When the land trade became available in the early 1930s, Scarborough led the board of trustees to buy Buckner's interest in the Dallas holding and then exchange the property for land just north of the original citrus orchard.[91] The Seminary then had a total of 1,200 acres of land for possible cultivation.

In 1934, in the midst of economic hardship, Scarborough called the orchard "the one hopeful financial resource to this institution."[92] Even though the fruit had been damaged by freezing temperatures more than once, the orchard paid consistently for a number of years. Scarborough even used the citrus land to help compensate faculty members who suffered through most of the 1930s on one-half salary. The land was valued at $500 per acre and was dispersed to professors to offset their lack of salary.[93]

The Southern Baptist Convention sanctioned a project in 1933 which eventually solved Southwestern's financial difficulties. The "Hundred Thousand Club" was a ten-year plan to reduce debts throughout the Convention by enlisting 100,000 people to donate one dollar per month beyond their normal gifts to the local church.[94] By 1944, just two years after Scarborough's retirement, the "Hundred Thousand Club" together with Cooperative Program monies had cleared the Seminary of its longstanding debt.[95]

The Seminary's endowment was forever a concern of L. R. Scarborough. He always held a grand vision for Southwestern and insisted that the Seminary move quickly to a vast future:

> Dr. Carroll made a broad platform, a titanic program for the Southwestern Seminary. His successors in this mighty task are trying to live up to his far-reaching leadership in building this institution. We feel that if we build small we will deserve to die. We cannot afford to sin against God, the future and a lost

Woman's Missionary Training School at Southwestern (now Barnard Hall).

world by not going out on a large program. To do otherwise is to court death.[96]

An ample endowment was a vital part of Scarborough's "large program."

Scarborough saw an intimate connection between the services offered by the Seminary and the obligation to endow it. Since Southwestern was missions-minded, evangelistic, and theologically sound, he reasoned, then the endowment would establish these virtues permanently on Seminary Hill.[97] He also tied the endowment to the distinctive denominationalism employed at Southwestern. A central focus of the institution was to develop denominational leaders of the "right sort." The Seminary was in the business of providing Southern Baptists with the best leadership Christianity had to offer. Southwestern was, Scarborough surmised, "the embodiment of Christian cooperation."[98] In his mind, he had fashioned on Seminary Hill an institution of denominationalism second to none.

By the time of Scarborough's retirement in 1942, his original goal of a $700,000 endowment had been reached and surpassed. The endowment fund totaled more than $1 million.[99] In addition, the Seminary was very near to canceling all of its existing debt.

When promoting the endowment program Scarborough could sum up his feelings about the Seminary in three words: "It is worthy."[100] Southwestern Seminary, he believed, was a denominational beacon for Southern Baptists and a substantial endowment would guarantee its continued usefulness.[101]

FINAL YEARS

Scarborough resigned as president of Southwestern Seminary on May 14, 1942.[102] Because of his advancing age he had by that time allowed the faculty, especially chairman of the faculty W. W. Barnes, to take over the basic operation of the Seminary.[103] According to Robert A. Baker, Scarborough had always given the faculty most of the responsibility for academics, while he concentrated on administrative matters.[104] In the final months, though, he looked to Barnes to oversee all areas of the Seminary's affairs.

Still, it was not easy for Scarborough to release the office of president. While he knew it was time to step aside, he was not sure how to let go of Southwestern. Indeed, it was impossible to completely detach himself from the denominational institution he had helped build. He explained:

> I cannot tell you how great a wrench to my soul it has been and is to separate myself from this noble band. When the vital blood stream of one's soul flows into a great institution, with its comrades, struggles and triumphs, it is no small task to turn the currents of that blood stream in another direction. Except for the necessity brought on by declining strength and age, a deep sense that the Seminary should have the highest service and the strongest vitalities of a strong leader, the hope of rendering further service in another direction for the dear Seminary, and for the consciousness that I am following the leadership of the Divine Spirit, I could not be strong enough to do what I am doing today.[105]

After twenty-seven years, Scarborough's presidency was at an end.

In his resignation speech, Scarborough pointed out six "vital fundamentals" of Southwestern. Two of those fundamentals expressed the denominationalism which had come to be so closely identified with Scarborough. In addition to "loyalty to Christ's churches," he mentioned the principle of "voluntary cooperation."[106] The cooperative spirit of Southern Baptists was one of the ideals championed by Scarborough in his long tenure as president.

Loyalty to the denomination and cooperation of individuals and churches were tenets to which Scarborough not only personally subscribed, but which he insisted that the Southwestern family hold to as well. He was so tenacious in his denominationalism that H. E. Dana suspected that Scarborough's "denominational loyalty has not been surpassed in the entire history of the Southern Baptist Convention."[107]

CONFLICT WITH J. FRANK NORRIS

Perhaps the unhappiest episode in Scarborough's career was his ongoing battle with J. Frank Norris (1877–1952).[108] Norris was the pastor of First Baptist Church in Fort Worth and in the

J. Frank Norris (1877–1952), pastor of First Baptist Church, Fort Worth, Texas.

Building a Seminary

early years had been a trustee of Southwestern Seminary. In fact, B. H. Carroll recommended Norris to the First Baptist pulpit committee in 1909.[109] Within two years of accepting the pastorate, however, Norris joined the ranks of Fundamentalism, and the denominational spirit he once possessed began to decay.

In the beginning, Norris fully supported the program of the Seminary. In addition to being a member of the board of trustees, he was instrumental in the choice of Fort Worth for relocation. But by 1911, after a revival experience in the North, Norris was determined to reshape the organization of First Baptist Church to support a more autocratic style of leadership.[110] In the same way, he hoped to control the work of the Tarrant Baptist Association, Southwestern Seminary, and (one might guess) the Southern Baptist Convention itself.

When Southwestern moved to Fort Worth, it was natural for the members of the faculty to become a part of the First Baptist congregation. By 1912, though, after Norris had been indicted for arson in connection with the church building, and as he raved the Fundamentalist line each Sunday, the faculty rapidly dispersed to other churches. Scarborough, who hoped to continue the seminal relationship between First Baptist and the Seminary, was the last to leave (in 1917).[111]

The 75 Million Campaign,[112] in which Scarborough served as director, and "modernism" at Baylor University became the igniting points in Norris' attacks on the Seminary and its president. The decade of the 1920s was the arena of battle between Scarborough's denominationalism and Norris' autocratic independence.

ORTHODOXY IN ACADEMIA

In 1921 Norris launched an assault on theological orthodoxy at Baylor University.[113] Samuel Dow, Norris asserted, should not have been allowed on the Baylor faculty because he believed in Darwinian evolution. Although Dow denied the charge, Norris continued his attack and soon included Baylor president S. P. Brooks in the foray.

Almost simultaneously, Norris asserted that W. W. Barnes, professor of Church History at Southwestern, was also an evolutionist.[114] Scarborough, who had already come to the defense of

Baylor, confronted Norris directly in defense of his colleague. The stage was set for a decade of conflict.

In the early 1920s, in response to Norris' criticism of S. P. Brooks, Scarborough presented a resolution to the Baptist General Convention of Texas in defense of the Baylor president.[115] At no time in the twelve-page document did Scarborough mention Norris by name. He was simply referred to as the "agitator."

S. P. Brooks, said Scarborough, was the very picture of theological orthodoxy.[116] In 1922 Brooks openly disagreed with the position of Samuel Dow, which for Scarborough was unequivocal proof that Brooks was no evolutionist.[117] The Baylor faculty, including Brooks, went so far as to draw up and sign a statement repudiating the theories of evolution in 1924.[118] In fact, Scarborough was himself so opposed to the teaching of evolution that had there been any doubt about Brooks, he may have been the one calling for his resignation.[119] Instead, Scarborough was convinced that Brooks was an innocent victim of Norris.

Even though an apology for Brooks, the statement did not overlook the difference in Scarborough's denominationalism and the independence of Norris. While the Tarrant Baptist churches which disfellowshipped Norris were described as "cooperating," the popular preacher Norris was portrayed in terms of destruction.[120] In addition, Scarborough liberally used the word "orthodox" in relation to practically every Baptist in Texas — with the exception of the "agitator."[121]

While the assault by Norris had begun at Baylor, he soon turned his attention to closer targets. Southwestern Seminary came under the preacher's scrutiny, and the Seminary president was particularly in the line of fire.

Norris was unusually concerned over money matters at the Seminary. This fixation was probably increased at the 1922 annual meeting of the Tarrant Baptist Association. Because of some changes in polity at the First Baptist Church (mainly an excessive amount of authority transferred to the deacons), the messengers were not seated.[122] Since Scarborough was instrumental in excluding First Church, Norris may have at that time decided to make stronger attacks on the president.

One of Norris' main queries dealt with a tract of land owned by Scarborough. Norris tried to prove that Scarborough bought ten acres of land adjacent to the Seminary campus before

Building a Seminary

Southwestern moved to Fort Worth and then maneuvered the Seminary into locating next to his own property.[123] Even if he failed to prove that, Norris also charged that the ten-acre plot was actually a part of the original tract donated to Southwestern by H.C McCart.[124] Actually, neither charge was true.

Scarborough did indeed own the ten-acre tract next to the campus. However, he bought the land from McCart in 1910 — the year after the Seminary decided to locate in Fort Worth.[125] Originally, McCart had reserved the land for his own use. After the Seminary decided on the site, though, and additional lands were purchased in the area, McCart sold the property to Scarborough. The record is clear that Scarborough did not own the ten acres until after the location of the Seminary had been settled.[126]

Still, as early as 1921 Norris had insisted that he be allowed to inspect Southwestern's financial records. In addition to the land fraud of which he accused Scarborough, Norris was convinced that discrepancies existed in the way Scarborough had used 75 Million Campaign monies. The Seminary president was confident that the financial records would show everything in balance and was more than happy for Norris to peruse the books. Scarborough wrote to his adversary:

> Of course, you will understand that giving you the privilege of going into the Seminary accounts and my personal and private business will carry with it the understanding that I will have the privilege with anybody whom I may select of going into the books and accounts of the First Baptist Church and your personal accounts. . . . When you come out to investigate the Seminary and me we will also go into some matters which I have information on concerning you and your work there. I am perfectly willing for the light to be thrown on anything out here that is necessary; and if it becomes necessary you will find me throwing some light on things down there, too.[127]

Norris never bothered to examine the Seminary accounts.

Another charge brought by Norris was that Southwestern had borrowed $2 million from the Foreign Mission Board.[128] In other words, he believed that money given expressly for missions had been diverted to the Seminary. Norris accused Scarborough of using his position as director of the 75 Million Campaign to channel additional monies into Southwestern.[129]

Once again, Norris was incorrect. While it was true that Scarborough was director of the 75 Million Campaign, he at no time had direct access to or control of the accounts. Instead, each state convention supervised the disbursement of Campaign funds.[130] In the same way, no monies were actually borrowed from the Foreign Mission Board. The Southern Baptist Convention in 1920 had agreed to loan the seminaries in Fort Worth, Louisville, and New Orleans monies designated to the Foreign Mission Board, Home Mission Board, and Education Board. The boards, then, were to be repaid by the surplus expected from the 75 Million Campaign.[131] In fact, less than $500,000 was given to the seminaries. Therefore, Norris was not only mistaken about the manner of the loan, but the amount as well.[132]

"The trouble is not with our books," Scarborough wrote. "The trouble is in another direction."[133] In the end the conflict was not over particular sums of money. Instead, Scarborough and Norris envisioned different directions for Southern Baptists.

DENOMINATIONALISM VS. INDEPENDENCE

Ecclesiology (ideas about the institutional church) was at the foundation of Scarborough's conflict with Norris. How does the local church function? Is it by cooperating with other churches in a denominational structure? Or does the local church act on its own and randomly choose which programs to support? While Scarborough was above all else a denominationalist, Norris operated more independently.

One example of Norris' anti-denominational spirit was his disdain of the Education Board.[134] He asked Scarborough:

> Do you think the raising of money in the name of missions and giving it to unscriptural institutions like the Education Board, which has now been practically repudiated by the Southern Baptist Convention — that this diversion of mission funds is true missionary work?[135]

Norris was equally incensed by the denomination's support of hospitals.[136] He had a rather narrow definition of how to use "mission funds."

As a confirmed denominationalist, Scarborough fought

Building a Seminary 47

against the idea of defunding Convention agencies and academic institutions. In addition, the support of hospitals, Scarborough believed, was a legitimate use of Southern Baptist monies. Norris "would close the doors of these healing institutions," he said. He would "send away . . . these sick people to die or to do the best they could."[137] For Scarborough, denominational funds spent on medicine helped the cause of Christ just as much as that spent on missions.

Scarborough was a leader in expelling Norris and the First Baptist Church from the Tarrant Baptist Association in 1922. The polity of the church had been changed to give full power to the pastor and deacons. Further, Norris had led the church into an isolationist stance that prevented any real cooperation with associational churches.[138] Scarborough stood against the independent nature of Norris' ecclesiology.

In January 1924 Norris wrote to Scarborough asking him to help First Baptist rejoin the Association.[139] Scarborough replied that he hoped all cooperating churches would hold membership in the Association—including First Baptist.[140] However, the question of church government remained unanswered and Scarborough was unsure about the willingness of Norris to truly cooperate.

> [I]t would be expected that any church to be in full co-operation with the Tarrant County Association would co-operate both in the Associational Mission Work together with the general denominational, state and Southwide mission and educational and benevolent program, and also the Hospital work. If your church comes into the Tarrant County Association these features of co-operation would be expected.[141]

Evidently, Norris was able to convince Scarborough that his attitude toward cooperation had changed. At the 1924 meeting Scarborough led a group which endorsed the readmittance of First Baptist.[142]

By the fall of 1924, however, Scarborough was again the leading opponent of Norris. When the Baptist General Convention of Texas met in Dallas, Scarborough led the way in unseating the messengers of First Baptist Church. His reasons were clear:

> The church sending these messengers for years has encour-

aged, financed, and otherwise supported a propaganda, state and southwide, which has cruelly and unjustly criticized, unmercifully misrepresenting and persistently opposed the program, method of work, institutions, causes, and elected and trusted leaders, fostered and promoted by this and the Southern Baptist Convention. Therefore the messengers of this church have no just rights to seats in this convention.[143]

Denominationalism won the day; the First Baptist messengers were expelled.[144]

The matter of a church governing itself as other Baptist churches was also of great concern to Scarborough. Norris was "irregular and unbaptistic" in his church polity.[145] In particular, Scarborough was disturbed by Norris describing himself as "Bishop" in First Baptist's Articles of Faith.[146] There are no bishops in Baptist life. Further, Scarborough was appalled that Norris allowed people to join his church who had not received believer's baptism.[147] In the mind of the denominationalist, this simply was not the way a Southern Baptist church should operate.

Still, in it all, Scarborough insisted that it was not his "purpose to put the First Baptist Church of Fort Worth out of business."[148] He was promoting denominationalism. Norris, he thought, was promoting something entirely different. While Scarborough may not have wanted to close First Baptist Church, he did want to expose the methods of J. Frank Norris.

THE FRUITS OF NORRISISM

In the late 1920s Scarborough published a tract in which he went on the offensive: "The Fruits of Norrisism."[149] In it Scarborough laid out his main objections to the methods of Norris. Again and again he reminded the reader that he was a denominationalist and Norris was not.

For Scarborough, "Norrisism" and "negativism" might have been interchangeable terms. After calling the movement a "cult," Scarborough lashed out at the negative spirit one could find within:

> It is anti-missionary and anti-institutional. It gives nothing to associational, state or home missions and only enough to foreign missions to get representation in the convention. It

spends most of its money on itself — some times in court trials for perjury, arson and murder, and in sending out free literature seeking to destroy the causes other people try to build.[150]

This was not just an exposition of "Norrisism," but a bold attack on Norris himself.

"Norrisism" is described by Scarborough as a fountain of hatred, a source of falsehood, an excuse for sensationalism, and against virtually everything. "It uses the pulpit," Scarborough lamented, "to vent its hatred against innocent personalities and institutions."[151] He never mentioned one redeemable quality about the man or the movement.

Scarborough went on to defend the Tarrant Association for excluding Norris and his church. In listing three "great principles," he came first to prove that denominationalism is the chief cause of the Association's action.

> The Tarrant County Association clearly recognizes the privilege of this church to refuse co-operation in building our mission causes, our schools, seminaries, hospitals and orphanages, but it denies them the right to come into fellowship of an association which is in favor of all these things and yet at the same time tries to decide the Association's course in supporting these institutions.[152]

For Scarborough there was no doubt: The followers of Norris "did not want to co-operate."[153]

As far as Scarborough was concerned, "Norrisism" did not represent the same Christianity that he did. The denominationalism that he fostered was hard to find in the Norris camp. In the final analysis, Scarborough felt he must defend that to which he had committed his whole life — the denomination.

The conflict between Scarborough and Norris raged in the 1920s and into the early 1930s. As the decade progressed, however, the warriors grew tired and each moved on to other interests. The two were never again on friendly terms, but the constant barrage diminished.

In the midst of controversy Norris had assured Scarborough that all would end well. "When you and I get to Heaven," he wrote, "we will have many good times sitting down and talking all these matters over."[154] One cannot be sure that Scarborough shared the sentiment. Still, the two rest today only a few hundred yards apart at Greenwood Cemetery in Fort Worth, and their conflict is left to historians.

SUMMARY

When B. H. Carroll brought Scarborough on to the faculty of Southwestern Seminary in 1908, it was clear that the young preacher from Abilene was a devoted Southern Baptist. No one could have imagined, however, that he would become the champion of denominationalism as the Seminary's second president. Perhaps Scarborough did not himself realize how much the denomination would come to mean in his personal and professional life.

Soon after occupying the "Chair of Fire," Scarborough led the campaign to secure monies for the move to Fort Worth. He was in his element. His powers of administration and his gift for fund-raising were evident as he worked with Carroll, the trustees, and the churches to obtain just the right tract of land and erect the Seminary's first building. Unknown at the time, Scarborough would soon be acting president. Denominational commitment fast became all-consuming.

It was in his twenty-seven-year tenure as president that Scarborough established himself as a premier denominationalist. W. W. Barnes, long-time professor of Church History at Southwestern, wrote that dedication to the denomination "became an obsession" for Scarborough.[155] The presidency became an official expression of his over-arching denominationalism. His Southern Baptist identity — or denominationalism — was everything to Scarborough.

There was never any doubt in Scarborough's mind that he was building a denominational institution. Soon after his inauguration as president he began to formulate a plan to transfer the Seminary to Southern Baptist ownership. He wanted Southwestern to be a school for *all* Southern Baptists. In his view, the Southwestern dream was too enormous for one state convention to encompass. He was building an institution for the entire Convention, and he laid the foundation for the denomination as a whole to participate in his venture.

Building a Seminary 51

When Scarborough spoke of the Seminary's endowment, the money was a secondary issue. Instead, the endowment was to insure the preservation of a denominational institution. An institution of the Convention — whether it be academic, medical, or missionary — was an invaluable asset. Southern Baptists must share his passion, he felt, for the continual existence of these institutions which served the cause of Christ so well.

In the same way, the conflict with J. Frank Norris was much more than a personality clash. It seemed to Scarborough that Norris stood against everything he himself believed. Norris and "Norrisism" were the embodiments of anti-denominationalism, and Scarborough was compelled to fight for the "co-operating churches." It was the spirit of denominationalism which drove him to push Norris out of the Tarrant Association and the Baptist General Convention of Texas. The conflict was between Scarborough the denominationalist and Norris the independent. In fact, he did not believe Norris was a Baptist at all.

As Scarborough progressed in his career at Southwestern, a new vision began to form in his mind. Total devotion to the denomination was a worthy obsession, but the progress of the denomination was even more important. The future of Southern Baptists called for a "New Denominationalism," and Scarborough was at the forefront of this progressive movement.

CHAPTER 3

Creating Something New

The national euphoria following World War I gave Americans a new vigor and sense of accomplishment. The experience of war taught the general populace that it was possible for great numbers of people to join together in a common cause and attain victory. The war had been brought to a successful conclusion, but the unity that resulted from the war effort continued. Americans quickly looked for new realms to conquer, and the religious world was included in the swelling tide of popular achievement.

While some sought to unite several religious groups in the "Interchurch World Movement,"[1] the leaders of the Southern Baptist Convention chose to concentrate on bringing a new unity to their own denomination. Less than one year after the war ended, Southern Baptists launched a bold program of evangelism and capitalization. Officially named the "Baptist 75 Million Campaign," this program forever changed the way Southern Baptists identified their convention and its mission.

In the beginning some leaders, including L. R. Scarborough, were opposed to the new Campaign. This broad unification, they felt, would lessen the sense of autonomy in the local church. Before long, however, almost everyone was convinced of the soundness of the program. For Scarborough, whose name became synonymous with the 75 Million Campaign, it was a chance to prove his denominational loyalty beyond any doubt. Because of his skills as an organizer and fund-raiser, Scarborough was invited to become general director of the Campaign and lead Southern Baptists into a new era. The 75 Million Campaign became the avenue of a "New Denominationalism" for Southern Baptists, and Scarborough became the spearhead of an innovative ideology.

The Campaign, which ran from 1919 to 1924, served as the forerunner and model of the Southern Baptist Cooperative Program. Scarborough structured the Campaign in such a way that churches and individuals contributed to the financial support of all denominational institutions at once. The Cooperative Program, initiated in 1925, was a natural result of the very successful 75 Million Campaign. Scarborough's leadership helped Southern Baptists invent a new method of gathering and distributing funds for missionary, educational, and benevolent causes.

Scarborough's New Denominationalism found expression in evangelism as well as convention structure. The 75 Million Campaign, however, was at the center of his fresh vision for Southern Baptists. Uniting the denomination for worldwide outreach was a dream he shared with all Campaign leaders. For Scarborough, the Campaign was the best way to re-create the Southern Baptist Convention into an archetype of his New Denominationalism.

CONVENTION STRUCTURE

Although the Southern Baptist Convention had not been constituted on the "society method," which calls for individual agencies to raise their own funds, prior to World War I it operated on somewhat of a society basis. Even though the Foreign Mission Board and Home Mission Board, for example, were under the Convention umbrella, they tended to appeal to local churches and individuals separately. The "convention method" called for a more unified approach to gathering funds.[2]

As early as 1900, some Baptists began to feel the need for a more holistic system in Convention operations. The "Committee on Co-operation" was formed in 1901 and recommended to the Southern Baptist Convention in New Orleans that the Convention exhibit more unity. Southern Baptists, reported the Committee, should aim "the energies of the denomination in one sacred effort."[3] The Committee hoped to unify the agencies, state conventions, and associations through its cooperative efforts. Recommendations for more unity were rejected in the 1901 meeting, however, and the idea of a centralized structure was laid aside for a number of years.

A breakthrough in consolidating Southern Baptist efforts came in 1917. The development of the "Executive Committee of the Southern Baptist Convention" brought the unity that was needed for the enlarged programs envisioned by Convention leaders. While the Committee was originally composed of seven members, by 1919 it included a president, a secretary, a representative from each Convention agency, and a member from each state in the Southern Baptist Convention.[4] Since it was empowered to act on behalf of Southern Baptists in the interim between Convention meetings, the Executive Committee gave a visible unity to the Convention that had not previously existed. Interestingly, W. W. Barnes credited the formation of the Executive Committee to the increased activity of laypersons in the Convention.[5]

By the end of World War I, then, the Southern Baptist Convention was operating in a new way. The unified effort of the Executive Committee was a precursor to the new direction Southern Baptists decided upon in 1919. In a very real sense, the 75 Million Campaign was the next logical step of a more united Convention.

When the idea of a program to raise several million dollars for Southern Baptist causes was first put forth, L. R. Scarborough had no idea he would be called upon to lead the endeavor.[6] Before the 75 Million Campaign was finished, though, Scarborough had imprinted his own personality and methods on the movement.

1919 CONVENTION

The Southern Baptist Convention of 1919 met in Atlanta, Georgia. It was a time of soaring emotions and fulfilled dreams as messengers still felt the elation of a victorious war.[7] J. B. Gambrell, president of the Convention, promised that the victory in Europe brought the world "to the dawn of a new era in civiliza-

Creating Something New 55

tion."⁸ He believed Southern Baptists should take the lead in shaping this new era. In his address to the Convention, Gambrell laid the foundation for a bold program of Southern Baptist advancement.

> It is, moreover, a conviction as deep as my soul that this Convention, representing the sentiments and convictions of millions of Christ's baptized people, ought to send out to our fellow Baptists everywhere a rallying call to unite to make effective in all lands the unique message of Christ and His apostles which we hold in trust for our brothers in every part of the world, to the end that humanity may be made free with the freedom wherewith Christ liberates individuals and nations.⁹

While not stating it directly, Gambrell was proposing a united financial program for Southern Baptists. A report soon came to the same Convention to launch the 75 Million Campaign.

In addition to membership on the Education Commission, Scarborough served on the "Committee on Financial Aspects of our Denominational Program." It was this committee that first suggested to the Convention a program to raise several million dollars for denominational causes. A. J. Barton of Louisiana submitted a resolution calling for the creation of a special commission to plan the fund-raising drive.¹⁰ It was Scarborough, though, who proposed the concluding statement of the "Committee on Financial Aspects":

> We recommend that a committee of one from each state be appointed by this Convention to plan in coöperation *[sic]* with the state agencies and the organized agencies of this Convention for a simultaneous drive to be taken each year in cash for a proportionate part of this $75,000,000, the campaign being so arranged that the part to be raised each year shall be larger than the year before, and thus secure the largest part the last year of the five.
>
> We further recommend that this committee in conference with the general Boards and the State Boards be requested to distribute the amounts among the different objects fostered by the Conventions and State Boards outside of local church support and apportion the amounts to the various states.¹¹

With the establishment of a "Campaign Commission" and recommendations on how to organize the program, Scarborough thought his part in the 75 Million Campaign was finished. He was soon to learn, however, that it had only begun.

CAMPAIGN COMMISSION

The Campaign Commission was given the responsibility of designing a strategy for raising funds. George W. Truett, pastor of the First Baptist Church of Dallas, Texas, was named chairman of the Commission.[12] Each state in the Southern Baptist Convention was represented with one member among the Campaign leaders.[13]

A planning session was set for June 4–5, 1919, at the First

Scarborough with George W. Truett, pastor First Baptist Church, Dallas.

Baptist Church of Atlanta. One of the main objectives was to decide how the $75 million was to be divided. In the end, missions received over half of the allotted funds and educational institutions received over $20 million.[14] Another feature of the meeting was to lay out a strategy for raising such a great sum of money. The Commission resolved to instigate a bold plan which called for the subscription part of the Campaign to be concluded by December 1919. In other words, they hoped to convince Southern Baptists to pledge $75 million in only six months.[15]

Perhaps the most important decision made at the initial meeting of the Campaign Commission was the election of a director for the program. The mind of the group turned almost immediately to L. R. Scarborough. He was well known not only for his deep devotion to the denomination, but also for his organizational skills. His efforts on behalf of Simmons College were public knowledge, and the leading role he played in the building of Southwestern Seminary was a prominent part of Scarborough's identity. After the meeting, George W. Truett wrote to Baptist newspapers that Scarborough was "one of the most prodigious toilers of his generation."[16]

Scarborough was not easily convinced that he should accept the position of general director of the Campaign.[17] He knew it would mean a long absence from Southwestern, and the Seminary remained his first calling. After prayer (and a good measure of persuasion from Commission members), he acquiesced and took the leadership responsibility. Scarborough remembered spending almost two days in prayer:

> I passed through the Garden of Gethsemane for hours. With a sense of unspeakable responsibility, heart-breaking and soul-oppressing, I finally found what I interpreted as God's will for me to accept the directorship of the campaign. Since then there has been a quiet peace and a sense of victory in my soul. Thus I throw myself out on the promises of God and the confidence of my brotherhood, to do my utmost to lead the forces to victory.[18]

Scarborough was now convinced that the Campaign would be successful. He wrote to Southern Baptists that the "power of God and a co-operant people" would push the Campaign to meet its goal.[19]

Truett was asked to tour as many states as possible to promote the Campaign.[20] Fulfilling speaking engagements and writing a few articles became his main tasks as chairman. He believed that Southern Baptists had entered a new era with the 75 Million Campaign. The enlargement of Convention programs, he felt, was a necessary part of moving the denomination to a place of real prominence in the religious world. Still, Truett realized that reshaping the Baptist identity was not an easy assignment. It was a new vision for the Convention, and helping people accept it was the responsibility of the Campaign Commission. "Henceforth," Truett wrote, "[Southern Baptists] must talk and think in millions."[21]

CAMPAIGN STRATEGY

The Sunday School Board building in Nashville was chosen as headquarters for the Campaign. Scarborough lived in Nashville for the last half of 1919 so that he could be directly involved in every facet of the new program.[22] On July 2 and 3 a second strategy meeting was held. This time First Baptist Church, Nashville, hosted the conference. It was a time of high emotions and grand-scale planning as more than 200 people met with Scarborough to organize the leadership and set dates for special emphasis.[23]

A four-level structure was decided upon. The central organization, with Scarborough at the helm, was located in Nashville. The second level was made up of the state conventions, as each state secretary/treasurer was looked to lead in the Campaign in his home region. Associations and local churches comprised the third and fourth levels of the Campaign structure.[24] Here Campaign coordinators and publicity directors represented the cause directly to the people.

The Campaign proper lasted only from July until December 1919.[25] During that time period, the organizational structure was set in place and the Campaign goal was promoted through newspapers and local churches. The climax of the Campaign was targeted for two Sundays: November 30 and December 7.[26] This eight-day period was named "Victory Week," and all pledges were to be made during this high point of the Campaign.[27] Individuals subscribed to a certain dollar amount, which was then to be paid over the five-year period, 1919–1924.[28]

Scarborough did not direct the Campaign as the lone occupant of the general director's office. There were at least fourteen others involved at the central level of organization.[29] Included on the general director's staff were B. C. Hening, assistant director; I. J. Van Ness, treasurer; Hight C. Moore, publicity director; Mrs. W. J. Neel, Woman's Missionary Union (WMU) director; and

*L. R. Scarborough,
c. 1920.*

T. B. Ray, survey director.[30] These people were responsible for their respective areas of the Campaign, but also served in an advisory capacity on virtually every aspect of the program.

At the heart of the Campaign strategy was a plan to reach every member of all churches in the Southern Baptist Convention. This was a new tactic for Baptists. Previously, prominent businessmen and wealthy deacons had been the targets of financial solicitation. In the 75 Million Campaign, however, the plan from the very beginning was to enlist all Southern Baptists to support the program.[31] This "common-man" strategy was integral to the New Denominationalism launched by the Campaign.

In 1919 there were 925 Southern Baptist Associations and almost 25,000 Southern Baptist churches.[32] The associational organization was set up very rapidly, with all 925 boasting an associational organizer, publicity director, and WMU organizer.[33] With few exceptions each of the 25,000 churches incorporated a local director (usually the pastor), a local organizer, and an organizer for the WMU. Scarborough had structured the Campaign so that each church had several "teams," consisting of "team captains" and "team workers."[34] It was this kind of intricate organization that characterized the entire Campaign.

Even Scarborough was amazed at the excitement that spread about the Campaign. It seemed that virtually every Baptist wanted to be involved. Scarborough held "co-operation" as one of the highest virtues, and in the 75 Million Campaign it greeted him at every turn. He described the unity:

> Everywhere there was co-operation. Nowhere was there opposition. The pastors, laymen, and women throughout the South took up the proposed organization, adopted it in their associations and churches, and began in a great, unified, co-operant way to arouse the people and put over the whole movement. The editors of the Baptist papers showed a most wonderful spirit of co-operation. They turned over to the Campaign all the force and power of their publications and threw themselves, without reserve, into the forward movement. Never was there seen such a harmonious and co-operating spirit among people. It was evident from the beginning that God in a mighty fashion had gripped the souls of Baptists throughout the South and united them for one high purpose and mammoth task.[35]

Suddenly, a more cooperative denomination sprang up around Scarborough and his Campaign staff.

The $75 million goal was only one part of the Campaign strategy. In addition to gathering money, Scarborough hoped to increase the membership rolls of Southern Baptists from three million to over five million. He wanted to see 5,000 decide upon a career in the ministry as a result of the Campaign. Most importantly for Scarborough, though, was a goal of two and a half million converts to the Christian faith because of the 75 Million Campaign.[36] People were equal in consequence to money in the program's goals.

"If money is all we get from the campaign," Scarborough wrote, "we have failed."[37] In addition to the millions of dollars and millions of people resulting from the Campaign, Scarborough believed the program would give Southern Baptists a new way to identify themselves. A growing sense of cooperation would encompass the entire Southern Baptist venture, Scarborough felt, and the end result would be an "aroused denomination."

Creating Something New 61

>Baptists will be compelled to make their plans larger, their programs greater to match their large and expanding opportunities, more efficient and effective their organization for reaching all their people with information, inspiration, organization and in order to meet the expanding responsibilities put on them by bigger programs.[38]

He saw a new kind of denomination emerging from the success of the 75 Million Campaign. The Southern Baptist Convention, in Scarborough's opinion, would not only embrace a greater number of people after the Campaign, but would itself be a greater enterprise.

CAMPAIGN PUBLICITY

The quality and amount of publicity circulated by the Campaign staff had never before been attempted in Baptist circles. In a matter of weeks, newspaper articles, pamphlets, posters, brochures, letters, and organizational charts flooded Southern Baptist states.[39] Baptist newspaper editors joined in the effort and gave ample space to Campaign promotion in almost every issue from July through December 1919.[40] Scarborough himself wrote numerous articles and several pamphlets, but he was aided by a ready staff of writers that helped trumpet the cause.

Realizing that the Campaign needed a slogan, T. V. Neal, Campaign organizer in Texas, proposed a phrase that at once caught the attention of everyone: "Millions for the Master" became the banner call of the 75 Million Campaign.[41] By the end of the summer of 1919, all promotional literature distributed by the central office in Nashville carried the slogan prominently. The maxim not only "charmed wherever it went," said Scarborough, but it just as easily "warmed the heart of the people."[42] The slogan conveyed the sentiment of everyone involved in the Campaign.

By September 1919, I. E. Reynolds, professor of music at Southwestern Seminary, had composed a Campaign hymn.[43] "When Millions Come Pouring In" incorporated the Campaign slogan and was sung, interestingly enough, to the melody of the "Battle Hymn of the Republic."

> A gift from ev-'ry Baptist in the south our aim shall be,
> We'll preach and talk and sing of Jesus' love so full and free,
> All up and down the land until the "Week of Victory,"
> When millions come pouring in.
>
> Chorus:
> Millions, millions for the Master,
> Millions, millions for the Master,
> Millions, millions for the Master,
> When millions come pouring in.[44]

Within a few weeks Reynolds' hymn was being sung on a regular basis in practically every Southern Baptist church. He cleverly placed new words with an already familiar tune, which enabled immediate identification with the song. The composition certainly had an effect on the millions "pouring in."

The first pamphlet issued by the Campaign was written by Southern Baptist Convention president J. B. Gambrell. "Facing a Worthy Task in a Worthy Way" set the tone of a large program reaching a vast amount of people.[45] T. B. Ray, survey director of the Campaign, quickly published "Evangelism—Enlightenment—Enlistment."[46] In it Ray outlined every mission, education, and benevolent cause to be supported by the Campaign. "There is enough work for all," he reminded his readers, and called on all Southern Baptists to join in reaching the goal.[47]

Scarborough gave the closing word in Ray's booklet. In doing so, he again challenged Baptists to adopt a new vision for the denomination. The 75 Million Campaign represented a new era for Southern Baptists, and Scarborough was committed to helping the Convention enter it.

> Above all things, Southern Baptists need to bind themselves to this larger life with indissoluble bonds. Indeed they need to build their life in a great manner into the expanding life of our Lord's spreading Kingdom. We need the expansion the raising of this 75 Million Dollars will enable us to share. This is our supreme opportunity for worthwhile participation in Christ's work in the world.[48]

For Scarborough, then, the 75 Million Campaign was much more than fund-raising. It was the encapsulation of a new method of operation for Southern Baptists.

Some of the Campaign publicity was of a lighter vein. A pam-

Creating Something New 63

phlet called "Soda Water, Cigars and Campaign Pledges," for example, presented the needs of the program with a humorous approach.[49] D. F. Green, corresponding secretary for Alabama, recounted a conversation with a friend who was unsure whether he could pay his Campaign pledge. Green noticed the gentleman smoked cigars and learned that he averaged four cigars a day. Green assured his friend that although he, too, enjoyed a good cigar, he could no longer afford to smoke because of his Campaign pledge. After a good deal of cajoling from Green, the man finally shouted, "Oh, shut up! . . . The pledge will be paid."[50]

"A Vital Discussion Between Two Business Men" was another less serious tract distributed by the Nashville office.[51] In this pamphlet the writer imagined a dialogue between two men involved in business dealings. While one was completely devoted to the Campaign cause, the other expressed reservations about committing to a five-year pledge. He was uncertain about the economic outcome of the years ahead. The first businessman was appalled that his associate would willingly trust banks and life insurance companies, yet not trust in divine providence to help him meet a Campaign pledge. "You ought to be ashamed of yourself," he admonished the man, "in being willing to do so much more for yourself than you are willing to do for God."[52]

As always, though, even in publicity Scarborough was more concerned with the weightier matters of the Campaign. "It is understood," he remarked, "that . . . every Baptist voice must sound out one note until the $75,000,000 campaign is put over."[53] A new degree of unity was needed, in Scarborough's opinion, for Southern Baptists to reach such a challenging goal:

> There must be unanimity and conformity, the sameness of program and organization. . . . There never was a time when Baptists needed to pull together as they do now. We must see eye to eye and face to face and move with a common motive and program. We should see a sacrifice of time and money and talent necessary to make victorious the campaign. . . . I, as General Director of the Campaign, am taking the position that no man or woman has any moral right to refuse to do what this movement demands of them.[54]

It was no longer a matter of mere money for Scarborough. It had risen to a question of morality. The Campaign had serious implications.

In the same way, he invited Baptists to share his concern for the more important matters of the program. He believed that the prayers of individuals would take on a deeper meaning because of the Campaign.[55] Baptists could experience a new confidence in divine care by their involvement. Christ's glory would become more evident as a result of the Campaign, Scarborough thought, and Christians would develop a new "love for the lost."[56]

Scarborough dreamed of tremendous results from the 75 Million Campaign. As he wrote publicity tracts and articles, he hoped to transmit his own enthusiasm to each reader. When every Baptist shared his dream, Scarborough supposed, then the greater vision of more denominational involvement would be realized.[57] He attempted to paint a mental picture of the Campaign's effect:

> Turn your imagination loose and give it wings and let it cross the seas and fly around the world and visit every land, go into the hospitals and those to be built, orphanages and those to be constructed, churches, Sunday schools, mission stations, and evangelistic meetings. Hear the joyous sound of new born souls by the millions coming to Christ, and the steady tread of a great force trained, cultured, going out to lead a lost world back to Christ.[58]

To a great extent, the publicity of the Campaign took on the excitement emanating from the general director himself.

CAMPAIGN ACTIVITY

Each month between July and November 1919 was set aside for a special emphasis in the Campaign. Since Scarborough did not meet with the leaders of the program until the first week of July, it was designated "Preparation Month."[59] August, "Information Month," was targeted for placing articles in Baptist newspapers, distributing the first Campaign pamphlets, and enlisting pastors to begin telling about the Campaign from the pulpit and in August revival meetings. "Intercession Month" in September was chosen for special emphasis on prayer. The WMU organizers named September 21–28 as a "week of prayer," and September 24 was particularly consecrated for all Southern Baptists to spend the day in intercession for the Campaign. October was "Enlist-

Creating Something New   65

ment Month." Here the focus was on enrolling new people in Sunday school and challenging young men and women to enter vocational ministry. In November, "Stewardship Month," special sermons on tithing were preached throughout the Convention.[60]

During "Enlistment Month," October 24 and 26 were especially significant days in the Campaign. On Friday, October 24, Baptist colleges and universities throughout the South held programs to lead students who believed themselves to be divinely called to enter full-time Christian service. Sunday, October 26, was set apart for the same purpose in churches.[61] An objective of the Campaign from the beginning had been to discover 5,000 people who were willing to commit their lives to the ministry.[62]

In preparation for what Scarborough called "Two Deathless Days,"[63] the Sunday School Board reprinted 25,000 copies of Scarborough's first book, *Recruits for World Conquests*.[64] In this book, one finds the first occurrence of Scarborough's term for bringing young people into vocational ministry: "Calling Out the Called." As a result of the book and the special programs on October 24 and 26, more than 6,000 persons submitted to a religious career.[65]

A spirit of revival sprang up in different areas as well. The initial goal was to convert two and a half million people to Christianity.[66] Reports came into the general director's office from a wide variety of churches telling of revival among Christians and persons led to salvation. A conservative estimate would be that thousands were added to Sunday school and church membership rolls as a result of the 75 Million Campaign.[67]

The opinion that the Campaign stood for more than money grew during the last half of 1919. I. E. Gates, for instance, was convinced that the Campaign was giving Southern Baptists a new vision. "We are going to be done with little plans and little faith," he wrote.[68] Gates felt that mission work on the foreign field, in particular, would be doubled or quadrupled because of the Campaign.

F. S. Groner, secretary of the Baptist General Convention of Texas, recounted a story of the increasing sense of denominationalism which grew out of the program:

> I preached at the First Baptist Church, McKinney, Sunday, and took dinner with one of the laymen. This church has a quota of

$140,000. Another layman in the church was also a guest in that home that day. I asked if they thought their church would raise its quota. One of the brethren exclaimed, "Raise our quota?" with emphasis that resented the implication that my question seemed to convey. The other brother said, "Why don't you ask if we are Baptists?"[69]

The Campaign was no longer a question of numbers of dollars raised, but one of loyalty to the denomination.

In the same way, Scarborough proclaimed with mounting excitement the news that "co-operation" was the defining point of the entire movement.[70] The cooperative spirit that he encountered in every quarter encouraged him to press the Campaign even further. "The co-operation we have had," he wrote, "... has been unstinted and unparalleled in all movements heretofore known in Baptist history."[71] For Scarborough, the growing cooperation among Southern Baptists was in itself enough to call the Campaign a success.

The six months of planning, strategy, and publicity by thousands of volunteers came to a climax at the end of November. With a Sunday on the front and back ends, "Victory Week" would decide the success or failure of the Campaign.

VICTORY WEEK

November 30 through December 7, 1919, was designated "Victory Week."[72] On these two Sundays, and in the week in between, pledges were gathered to meet the five-year $75 million goal. Scarborough always believed the goal should have been set at $100 million.[73] Still, everyone involved in the Campaign would have been satisfied to meet the stated goal.

"The Baptist pot is boiling," Scarborough declared. "Put fuel to the fire. Create the 'Will to Work and Win.'"[74] He realized that everything depended on the climactic week of victory. While he believed that ultimate victory was dependent on divine action,[75] he also knew that human endeavor was a necessary part of success. Scarborough never retreated from reminding Southern Baptists that their activity was as important as their prayers. "Every church organized now, every church mobilized now, every church informed now" was a message he kept sending to the Baptist constituency.[76]

While "Victory Week" may not have been the greatest event since Pentecost (as Scarborough stated),[77] it was nevertheless a tremendous success for the Convention. By the end of the first day, November 30, over $54 million had been pledged to the Campaign.[78] By the following Sunday, which marked the end of "Victory Week," the goal had been exceeded by more than $1 million.[79] The 75 Million Campaign had indeed been successful.

The *Baptist Standard* of December 2, 1919, touted headlines such as "North Carolina Pressing on to Victory"; "Good for Virginia"; "Memphis Man Gives $400,000"; and "FBC of Dallas with Quota of $300,000 Gives $575,000 First Day." The triumph of the Campaign was due to both large and small donations. Churches like Broadway Baptist in Fort Worth, Texas, and Southside Baptist in Birmingham, Alabama, raised more than $200,000 each.[80] On the other hand, a blind girl in Macon, Georgia, gave her pastor all the money she had — a single dollar bill.[81]

Because of inclement weather during "Victory Week," Scarborough chose to extend the subscription period for two additional weeks.[82] The $75 million goal was left farther and farther behind with each progressing day. By Sunday, December 13, the total exceeded $81 million.[83] By the end of the Campaign, more than $90 million had been pledged for Southern Baptist missions, education, and benevolence.[84]

The Campaign succeeded far beyond what most people dared to dream. The millions of dollars meant a greater outreach for the Convention. Still, though, it was not the amount of money that most impressed Scarborough; it was the effect on the lives of individual Baptists. "Probably the most meaningful and significant triumph of all the Campaign," he said, "is found in the mighty spiritual awakening in the hearts of our people."[85] The denomination had changed because of the 75 Million Campaign.

CAMPAIGN FOLLOW-UP

In February 1920 Scarborough met with representatives from the Executive Committee, state conventions, Baptist newspapers, and the Campaign Commission in Nashville.[86] Reports were made on the progress of the Campaign and the need for continuing efforts in gathering pledges. Scarborough was asked to continue his role as general director. While the Campaign was over for some, there still remained several years of labor for Scarborough.

The final tally of money pledged to the Campaign was $92,630,923.[87] The dollar total and unified efforts of Southern Baptists had a positive effect on the whole Convention. Millard Jenkins, Campaign organizer for Georgia, commented:

> The Campaign has brought us closer unity among ourselves as a denomination. Each Baptist church is sovereign in its own independence. There is nothing to unite Baptist churches as a great denomination but their cooperative work.[88]

As for Scarborough, he was thankful to God that "co-operancy and His power won" the Campaign victory.[89]

By the time of the annual meeting of the Southern Baptist Convention in May 1920, Scarborough had prepared a Campaign Commission report to deliver to the messengers.[90] The Convention came to a peak of intensity as George W. Truett, chairman of the Campaign Commission, presided over the special presentation. George W. McDaniel of Virginia, a member of the Commission, addressed the assembly on behalf of the 75 Million Campaign; B. C. Hening, assistant general director, offered a prayer of thanksgiving; and Scarborough himself read the official Campaign report to the Convention.[91]

Scarborough began the report with an overview of the previous year's activity. He briefly recounted the decision in Atlanta to launch the Campaign, the organization of June and July 1919, and the efforts leading to "Victory Week."[92] In addition to announcing the grand total of pledges, Scarborough was able to report that more than $12 million in cash was already in hand.[93] In terms of dollars, the Campaign was a tremendous success.

The vast amount of money, though, was not all that Scarborough wanted to report. He believed that "spiritual and denominational enrichment" were equal consequences of the Campaign.[94] Convention unity, a greater vision for the denomination, and a new level of stewardship were only some of the evidences of denominational enrichment. For Scarborough, the Campaign brought an unprecedented unanimity among the churches:

Creating Something New 69

> The Campaign has cemented Southern Baptists into a mighty, mobilized, spiritual phalanx from Maryland to Mexico and from Florida to Missouri. Our people see eye to eye and walk in the unison of a common faith as never before. Southern Baptists offer a solid front of aggressive Kingdom workers. The accomplishment of a great task together has produced a mighty Baptist solidarity.[95]

The Convention was united as never before, in Scarborough's opinion. Southern Baptists were now ready to become a world-force in evangelism, missions, and education. The 75 Million Campaign, Scarborough felt, had produced a renewed emphasis on Christian service throughout the whole Convention.

E. C. Routh, editor of the *Baptist Standard*, penned a glowing commentary on Scarborough's report:

> One of the highest hours of the Convention came Thursday afternoon, when Dr. L. R. Scarborough read the report of the 75 Million Campaign Commission.... What an eventful year since our last meeting in Atlanta! How marvelous has been the leadership of our God! The gifts, amounting to more than $92,000,000, were not so significant as the enlistment of thousands of our choicest young men and women in special Kingdom service. The pulse-beat of the Campaign was felt to the ends of the earth. Tens of thousands were led to Christ, and we had last year the largest increase in our membership in the history of Southern Baptists.[96]

Routh agreed with Scarborough: The 75 Million Campaign had increased the effectiveness of the denomination.

The Campaign Commission realized that an organized program to continue the denominational momentum was a necessary part of the work. Scarborough offered four recommendations to the Convention messengers.[97] First, he advised local churches to stay up-to-date on pledge collection. Second, Scarborough hoped that the evangelistic emphasis would continue throughout the South. The third recommendation was for a drive to press every Baptist to subscribe to his or her state newspaper. In addition, Scarborough called on the Convention to increase the enrollment at Baptist colleges and universities. Finally, Scarborough recommended a committee be appointed to insure the "conservation of the victories already won."[98] This was the beginning of the "Conservation Commission," with Scarborough as chairman.[99]

The 75 Million Campaign itself had been brought to a successful conclusion. The monetary goal was exceeded by more than $17 million. With more than $12 million already banked, the prospects in May 1920 seemed bright. Yet, there was still a great deal of work that remained for Scarborough and his new Commission.

CONSERVATION COMMISSION

Scarborough served as chairman of the Baptist 75 Million Campaign Conservation Commission from 1920 through 1925.[100] While he had resided in Nashville for the six months of the Campaign, he returned to Fort Worth in December of 1919 to resume his duties as president of Southwestern Seminary. From his office on Seminary Hill, Scarborough directed the work of the Conservation Commission for over four years.

Raising $92 million in pledges was not enough for Scarborough. He continued to see the Campaign as an "unfinished task."[101] By 1921, however, an economic recession was manifesting itself throughout the United States.[102] The faltering economy became an enemy that the Conservation Commission battled against for the remainder of its existence. Even though $22 million in cash had been collected by 1921, the pledge amount seemed more and more distant.[103]

Scarborough was determined to gather as much of the pledged money as possible. "Do you love our schools . . . our mission boards," he asked Baptists in Texas. "God help us to put it over!"[104] He connected the Campaign goal with the denominational identity of Southern Baptists and insisted that the drive be completed.

The Conservation Commission continued to publicize the Campaign through newspaper articles and pamphlets. One of the tracts Scarborough wrote at this stage, "What You Have Missed,"[105] was aimed at those who had not yet committed to the 75 Million Campaign. He told readers that they were excluding themselves from a "glorious forward task." In typical fashion Scarborough asked for cooperation and involvement in the Campaign. Christ had given his life for each of them, Scarborough reminded his readers. "You give your life and your best," he wrote, "and if need be die to do it."[106] This was serious business.

Creating Something New

Scarborough also continued speaking about the Campaign at every opportunity. Addressing the executive board of the Baptist General Convention of Texas in 1924, he proclaimed again the essence of the program. "Our Baptist program is a unified program," he said.[107] Scarborough called on the board to be cooperative in their own churches and among Texas Baptists as a whole. "Every Baptist church needs every other Baptist church," Scarborough declared. A decision not to cooperate was never positive in Scarborough's mind. It was a question of whether to cooperate with other Baptists, or to totally retreat from denominational involvement. Scarborough instructed the board: "Noncooperation and isolation are suicidal to any preacher, church, school, or other institution. Cooperation with your brethren is . . . the way of success."[108] The longer the 75 Million Campaign lasted, the more Scarborough tied it to the cooperative efforts of all Southern Baptists.

Even with the concerted efforts of Scarborough and Frank Burkhalter, publicity director for the Conservation Commission, receipts continued to dwindle. In the fall of 1922 Scarborough petitioned the help of Southern Baptist pastors:

> We have lost during the Campaign so far, through death, removals and business failures, many thousands of our Campaign pledges. We ought to make these up by getting subscriptions from the members not heretofore subscribing. This matter is largely up to the pastors. They hold, with their faith, their prayers, their aggressive leadership, this movement in their hands and hearts. If they push it, it will go over. Otherwise, we will fail.[109]

In the final analysis, Scarborough believed, the success of the Campaign depended on the devotion of Baptist pulpiteers.

By 1924 Scarborough realized that not even the original $75 million goal would be met. By July, only a little more than $53 million had been received.[110] But even that amount of money was enough to help the Convention expand considerably during the time of the Campaign. For example, while only 680 new churches were started from 1914 to 1919, more than 2,200 churches were established during the five years of the program.[111] In addition, Southern Baptist Foreign Missions had spread from only nine countries, prior to the Campaign, to seventeen countries by

1924. There were gains on every front. The Home Mission Board increased its program, Baptist colleges were improved, and orphanages had become better equipped.[112]

By any estimation the Campaign was a tremendous success for Southern Baptists. Scarborough's first biographer, H. E. Dana, did not count the Campaign as a failure. For Dana, the 75 Million Campaign had "created in Southern Baptist consciousness the vision of a great task."[113] He thought this accomplishment enough to deem the Campaign victorious in every way.

As the work of the Conservation Commission drew to a close, Scarborough focused more and more on the "by-products" of the Campaign.[114] While receipts had fallen short of the expected $92 million, Scarborough saw other results of the program as equally important. The unity of Southern Baptists and the improved organization in the denomination were evidence to him that the Campaign had been good for the Convention. Perhaps most important, though, was that Southern Baptists were now less provincial and more outwardly directed. "The Campaign," Scarborough wrote, "has made Southern Baptists more nearly horizonless Christians. They have learned to see anew the lost world."[115]

At the 1925 annual meeting of the Southern Baptist Convention, Scarborough gave the Conservation Commission's final report.[116] Pledges had exceeded the original goal by $17 million and actual receipts totaled the same amount under the stated goal. The final tally was $58,591,713.[117] Scarborough again pointed to the progress achieved by the Campaign. He applauded Southern Baptists for the increases in missions, hospital care, education, and orphanages. Still, Scarborough could not resist one reflection on the financial failure when he referred to the "27,000 supposedly co-operating churches."[118] In the end, though, he knew the Campaign had caused the Convention to move into a new era. "Southern Baptists will never be what they were," Scarborough asserted.[119]

RESULTS OF THE CAMPAIGN

The 75 Million Campaign had forever changed the way Southern Baptists viewed themselves and their participation in the world. Scarborough did not see himself as the creator of the

Creating Something New

new age for Baptists, but looked to Christ and the collaborative effort of the whole Convention.

> I did not in any way desire or seek the leadership you put upon me in the 75 Million movement. I never at any time felt worthy of your confidence, equal to the task, nor in any sense do I merit the praise for the successful achievements of the Campaign. I have felt all along the urge of God's will, the consciousness of Christ's presence, the assurance of victory through His power and for His glory. Whatever of success in achievement we have made together in these glorious years, the honor and glory belong first to Christ for His wonderful leadership and provident mercy, and next to our co-operating forces who so gloriously threw themselves into the battle and continued so faithfully through the years. My part in it all has been small. I only gave my little life the best I could. I crave none of the honor or praise.[120]

Perhaps, though, Scarborough was being too modest. Before 1919 he was known as the president of Southwestern Seminary. Because of his leadership in the Campaign, however, "Scarborough" had become a "household word throughout the entire Southland."[121] In the minds of Southern Baptists, the 75 Million Campaign and L. R. Scarborough were virtually one and the same.

The Campaign brought advances in every area of the Southern Baptist Convention. Academic institutions, hospitals, orphanages, and mission agencies were left with larger programs and a broader vision for the future. There was no doubt among Southern Baptists that the Campaign had altered the organization and effectiveness of the Convention. Two features in particular had a lasting impact on the Southern Baptist Convention: a New Denominationalism and the Cooperative Program.

NEW DENOMINATIONALISM

Although Scarborough had accepted the leading role in the Campaign reluctantly, by mid-June of 1919 he was fully committed to the program and completely devoted to the office of general director. Soon the Campaign began to reflect Scarborough's own organizational style. The publicity, structure, and progress of the Campaign all emanated from the unique leadership of L. R. Scarborough.

It was through the comprehensive nature of the 75 Million Campaign that Scarborough helped Southern Baptists formulate a New Denominationalism. The Convention changed dramatically from 1919 to 1925. Sunday school enrollment increased 132 percent, and total dollars donated to missions and benevolence causes rose almost 200 percent.[122] There was a brand new kind of unity among Southern Baptists, and, as Scarborough broadcast, the Convention would never be the same.[123] A new spirit of denominationalism captured the imaginations of those involved in the Southern Baptist cause.

In his history of the Campaign, *Marvels of Divine Leadership*, Scarborough devoted a chapter to "Campaign By-Products."[124] While the $92 million pledge was certainly a significant matter, Scarborough witnessed other results stemming from the Campaign. The first and most important by-product for Scarborough was the "New Denominationalism."

> Southern Baptists as never before have been convinced of their unified and denominational strength. The consciousness of world power has come upon them; the bonds of denominational life have been strengthened. This does not mean an emphasis upon so-called sectarianism — not that by any means — but the unification and solidarity of the forces making up the people called Baptists.[125]

The unity of denominationalism had swept up Southern Baptists during the 75 Million Campaign. Not only had the Campaign given Baptists a new way to gather and distribute funds, but it had actually re-created the way Southern Baptists identified themselves. After the 75 Million Campaign, they were a unified whole — a *denomination* — as never before.

Part and parcel of the New Denominationalism was a renewed vision of reaching the entire world with the Gospel. The Campaign helped Southern Baptists accept as a personal obligation the responsibility of supporting missions around the globe. "They have heard anew," Scarborough recorded, "the voices of God and all humanity calling them in unselfish service."[126] It was the duty of Southern Baptists in particular, they now felt, to fulfill the Great Commission. The New Denominationalism involved a

Creating Something New 75

new measure of obedience to the Baptist way, and the Convention wanted to share its doctrines with as many people as possible.[127]

Scarborough made cooperation the one recurring theme of the 75 Million Campaign. A higher level of cooperation among Southern Baptist churches was a necessary ingredient if the New Denominationalism was to endure. Yet, it was not just a cooperative spirit in general that Scarborough championed, but a singularly denominational cooperation. If Christ's Kingdom was to be manifest in every part of the world, he acknowledged, then churches of "like faith and order" had to work together.[128] For Scarborough, the emphasis was on an expressly *Southern Baptist* denominationalism.

For a church or an individual Baptist to refuse the cooperative method was "heresy" to Scarborough.[129] He believed that the cause of Christ could easily be doomed if cooperation were rejected. "The whole scheme of putting over the program of Jesus Christ in its theoretical and doctrinal side is dependent upon the doctrine of co-operation," he wrote.[130] The New Denominationalism among Southern Baptists could only survive if the entire Convention pulled together in one mutual venture.

The 75 Million Campaign had proven that a unified program of denominational fund-raising was the most efficient system available. Although cooperation was an indispensable part of the New Denominationalism, Scarborough was committed to a particular form of cooperation: Southern Baptists had to support the whole program of the Convention and not designate funds to favorite causes. Scarborough called this kind of partisanship "lop-sided cooperation."[131] Designated gifts defeated the very purpose of the Campaign. Scarborough saw very little difference between "lop-sided cooperation" and a refusal to cooperate entirely. "It is partial, selective, self-willed, prejudiced cooperation," he complained.[132] In order for the New Denominationalism to continue, Southern Baptists had to entrust monetary gifts to the Convention program as a whole.

The New Denominationalism was also evident in 1925, when Southern Baptists adopted their first confession of faith. Scarborough served on the "Committee on Baptist Faith and Message" and wanted to insure that a statement on cooperation was prominently placed in the document. He wrote a draft of "Article 19 on

Co-operation."[133] While the final manuscript placed "co-operation" as Article 22 and stated the doctrine in different words, there is an unmistakable affinity between the two documents.[134] Scarborough had safeguarded the New Denominationalism by helping to make "co-operation" an official part of the Southern Baptist confession of faith.

The spirit of cooperation became closely identified with Scarborough. Jeff Ray, professor of homiletics at Southwestern Seminary during Scarborough's presidency, contended that cooperation and Scarborough were almost inseparable. "So often and so earnestly has he used the unusual word 'co-operant,'" Ray wrote, "that many people think he coined the word."[135] For Scarborough, cooperation embodied the purpose of the 75 Million Campaign and, indeed, the very essence of the New Denominationalism.

COOPERATIVE PROGRAM

The Southern Baptist Cooperative Program was established in 1925 as an outgrowth of the 75 Million Campaign.[136] As the close of the Campaign drew near, Convention leaders hoped to continue the advances made through the unified program. A "Future Program Commission" was named in 1924, which made recommendations to the 1925 annual Southern Baptist Convention for a financial program similar to the 75 Million Campaign.[137] Interestingly, the first report on the Future Program immediately followed Scarborough's final report on the Campaign.[138] The two programs were intimately linked in thought and practice.

The Future Program Commission chose the name "The Cooperative Programs of Southern Baptists."[139] It was a program which incorporated every facet of Convention work. With the 75 Million Campaign as the model, the Cooperative Program united all Southern Baptist causes under one system. While Scarborough's Campaign had been the birthplace of the New Denominationalism, the Cooperative Program gave it a permanent home.

The same kind of cooperation that Scarborough proposed was put forth by the Future Program Commission. They, too, called for loyalty to the denomination as a whole.

Creating Something New 77

> While we recognize the right of individuals and churches to designate their gifts, we urge most insistently that contributions be made to the whole program and that pastors and denominational representatives . . . impress upon the people the importance of unity in its support.[140]

The Commission hoped that the unanimity which resulted from the 75 Million Campaign would continue in the new program. Commitment to a single purpose by all Southern Baptists, they concluded, was the way to advance the denomination even further.

The Cooperative Program gave Southern Baptists a lasting denominational unity.[141] The financial arrangements inaugurated in the 75 Million Campaign, and proven by five years of testing, found abiding expression within the Convention structure.[142] Methods forged in the 75 Million Campaign became common practice for Southern Baptists. Through the auspices of the Cooperative Program, the New Denominationalism initiated by Scarborough and the Campaign Commission shaped the activity of the Convention for most of the twentieth century.

SUMMARY

The creation of the Executive Committee in 1917 paved the way for the 75 Million Campaign. In addition, World War I gave all Americans a cohesion that had not been known since the Civil War separated the Union. By the dawn of the 1920s, then, Southern Baptists were ready to enter a new era of cooperation and unity.

The 75 Million Campaign was a bold venture. Not only had Baptists never raised such a large sum of money, they had never before been willing to yield to the full meaning of existing as a denomination. The autonomy of local churches and freedom of conscience among individual Baptists were so jealously guarded that the unified work of the denomination was hampered. Following the war, however, the time was right for new methods and daring objectives. The 75 Million Campaign was the right program at the right moment in Southern Baptist history.

Even though L. R. Scarborough was originally skeptical about the Campaign, he soon converted to a zealous advocate of the movement. George W. Truett and his Campaign Commission recognized the uncommon combination of skills possessed by the president of Southwestern Seminary. Scarborough not only had fund-raising experience and talent, but he also exhibited a keen adeptness for organization. When the Commission considered possible candidates for general director of the Campaign, it was soon a unanimous conclusion that Scarborough was the only choice.

Scarborough quickly gave the Campaign a touch of his own personality. Publicity rang with the sound of Scarborough's voice as every feature of the Campaign proclaimed the dogma of denominational loyalty. It was more than a request for commitment to the Southern Baptist cause. Scarborough demanded complete devotion to the Campaign, because in so doing, every Southern Baptist declared his love for Christ and his church. The 75 Million Campaign became for Scarborough an expression of individual and corporate faith.

It was impossible for Scarborough to completely conceal his disappointment over the monetary shortfall. He praised the Convention as a whole for its untiring efforts, but chided local churches for failing to meet their goals.[143] Still, he was more concerned with the achievements of the Campaign. In the end, Scarborough did not see millions of dollars, but denominational unity, as the main object of the program. Southern Baptists had become a different people because of the Campaign, and in Scarborough's view that balanced all accounts.

Scarborough began and ended the Campaign with the word "co-operation." He was continually amazed at this new spirit among Southern Baptists. In the past, the interdependence of churches was a secondary matter. But with the introduction of the 75 Million Campaign, Baptist churches throughout the South fully realized the need for denominational connection. The exhilaration of $92 million in pledges caused Southern Baptists to acknowledge the importance of a united effort by the entire Convention.

The fresh sense of loyalty, commitment, and cooperation pushed the Southern Baptist Convention to experience a New Denominationalism. Scarborough himself recognized that this new Convention unity was a result of the 75 Million Campaign.[144] The Campaign caused Southern Baptists to identify themselves

Creating Something New

more readily as a denomination with a world-vision and a global mission.

Scarborough may not have comprehended his role in developing the New Denominationalism. As general director of the Campaign he shaped the organization and message of the program. In turn, the 75 Million Campaign gave the Convention a new revelation of its purpose and identity. The Campaign, in effect, created a New Denominationalism among Southern Baptists. In addition, the Cooperative Program — a natural result of the Campaign — has fostered the New Denominationalism for the better part of the twentieth century. While he may not have been willing to admit it himself, there is a direct link between Scarborough and the New Denominationalism.

The 75 Million Campaign was indeed at the heart of the new Convention structure. Even the Campaign itself, though, was concerned with more than money. The number of people reached with the Christian message became just as important as the number of dollars collected. For Scarborough, the evangelistic endeavors of churches and individuals was an equally vital part of the New Denominationalism.

CHAPTER 4

Giving a New Direction

A broad spirit of evangelism has always been a hallmark of Southern Baptists. At the genesis of the Convention in 1845 the ideological center was foreign missions, with an emphasis on winning converts to the Christian faith. A common wish to see individuals and nations turned toward Christ became the bond that unified the Southern Baptist Convention.

The religious experience of L. R. Scarborough was characterized by the Baptist zeal for evangelism. From the influence of his parents, who were both fully committed to personal evangelism, to the Christian fervor of B. H. Carroll, Scarborough was invested with a lifelong enthusiasm for sharing his witness of the Savior. It was an enthusiasm that pervaded his private life, as well as his professional career.

Perhaps as much as anything else, evangelism was the centerpiece of the New Denominationalism. For Scarborough, the purpose of strengthening Southern Baptist institutions was so that each of them could more effectively reach the world with the Gospel. In the 75 Million Campaign, for example, Scarborough insisted that the money collected was only important if it represented the number of people that could be added to the membership of Southern Baptist churches. Scarborough felt that the Campaign would have been a failure if it only produced a larger

Scarborough in Southwestern president's office.

income. A New Denominationalism was created by the 75 Million Campaign, but in Scarborough's estimation the validation came in the Campaign's evangelistic emphasis.

It is significant that Scarborough never relinquished his professorship in evangelism. Even after becoming the president of Southwestern Seminary, he continued to hold his classes in evangelism on a regular basis. B. H. Carroll envisioned the "Chair of Fire" as a main component in the Seminary's curriculum. In choosing Scarborough as the first occupant of that Chair, Carroll insured that evangelism would remain an important feature for students at Southwestern. Scarborough never saw his professorship as secondary to his presidency. Rather, each role accomplished the same objective: training and graduating Southern Baptist ministers who believed in evangelism as much as he did.

In the same way, Scarborough aimed his published writings at evangelistic targets. He produced sixteen books from 1914 through 1942. While a few books focused on other areas (*Marvels of Divine Leadership* recounted the 75 Million Campaign, for instance), the majority of his works dealt with evangelistic themes. Of Scarborough's first four books, three centered on strategies for more practical and effectual methods for Southern Baptists to use in evangelism.[1] The theories that he put forth in the classroom were intertwined with the theses of his books. Evangelism became for Scarborough not just a personal obligation, but a professional responsibility.

Interestingly, Scarborough was just as concerned about enlisting young Christians for vocational ministry as he was about winning converts to Christianity. He termed this endeavor "Calling Out the Called" and made it a recurring theme of his message to Southern Baptists. He was convinced that more people must enter the ranks of Baptist preachers, evangelists, and missionaries if the Convention was to reach its full potential. In the classroom and in his writings, Scarborough tied evangelism and evangelistic training to the growth of Southern Baptists. For Scarborough, then, evangelism became the way to nurture the New Denominationalism.

A NEW THRUST IN EVANGELISM

Although evangelism was already a main focus of the Southern Baptist Convention, it became more fully organized in the early twentieth century.[2] The Southern Baptist Home Mission Board was especially interested in furthering evangelistic causes throughout the United States, particularly in the South. At the annual meeting of the Southern Baptist Convention in 1906, the Home Mission Board was empowered to develop a department of evangelism. Interestingly, B. H. Carroll, who served as Scarborough's mentor in evangelistic method, addressed the Convention urging the adoption of this new program in evangelism.[3]

William Wister Hamilton was chosen as the Home Mission Board's first "general evangelist." He served in this capacity from 1906 until 1909.[4] During the summer months of 1908, several conferences were instigated by Hamilton to promote a program of personal evangelism. One of these meetings was held at Hot Springs, Arkansas, where L. R. Scarborough was a featured speaker. Topics ranging from preparation for revival to follow-up on

Giving a New Direction 83

new Christians were presented during a three-day period.[5] This was one of the first appearances by Scarborough as Southwestern Seminary's professor of evangelism, and he entered the conference with characteristic enthusiasm.

Ten years later, in 1918, Scarborough returned to Hot Springs to address the annual meeting of the Southern Baptist Convention. Just as B. H. Carroll challenged the Convention of 1906 to increase its evangelistic efforts, Scarborough called on Southern Baptists to reevaluate their commitment to denominational evangelism. The address made such an impact that the Home Mission Board decided not only to publish the speech in tract form but also to increase the efforts of its Department of Evangelism.[6]

Scarborough began the address with nine points which characterized personal evangelism in the Southern Baptist Convention. He mentioned the endeavors of Sunday school workers, evangelism-minded pastors, and associational missionaries, as well as the hundreds of "independent evangelists" who traveled throughout the South. He was careful, though, to credit the Home Mission Board's Department of Evangelism as the "largest single organization in the field resulting in the largest returns."[7]

The Home Mission Board evangelists certainly had a tremendous influence on the work of Southern Baptist churches. Scarborough reported that since the Department of Evangelism's inception in 1906, its representatives were responsible for more than 85,000 baptisms and almost 120,000 new members in Southern Baptist churches.[8] Even though World War I had caused a decrease in activity, Scarborough pushed the Convention to reach for higher goals in evangelism.

For Scarborough, seven elements composed the "Truest Kind of Evangelism." In addition to biblical and doctrinal standards, he thought, Southern Baptist evangelism ought to be "denominational." When a person becomes a Christian, Scarborough said, "he should be anchored to something."[9] That something, of course, was the Southern Baptist Convention. Further, he said, evangelism must receive its power from the divine source available through the Holy Spirit.

Perhaps the most important element for Scarborough was the one he named last: "recruiting evangelism."

> Leaders are needed now more than ever before in the ministry and in missions and in all religious phases of the . . . work. God is calling men into His harvest. We should call them out, and in the hours and spirit of soul-winning is the best time to do it. . . . So let us in our evangelism greatly strengthen our spiritual leadership in all the phases of Kingdom activities. Win souls, build souls, call out leaders.[10]

The idea of recruiting young people for vocational ministry was central to Scarborough's message. He saw in the next generation of leaders the forces needed to continue the New Denominationalism.

The excitement generated by the 75 Million Campaign gave a new intensity to Southern Baptist evangelism. Scarborough set a daring goal for the Campaign to produce two and a half million converts and 5,000 new preachers.[11] While the first goal was not reached, the second was exceeded as over 6,000 high school and college students pledged to enter the ministry. The Campaign led to a peak in evangelistic fervor that the Convention had never before experienced.

By the 1921 annual meeting of the Southern Baptist Convention, the call for evangelistic emphases was heard in every quarter. J. L. Gross of Texas, for example, proposed that Southern Baptists "put on a campaign of personal soul-winning at least just as thorough, well organized, and far-reaching as was the 75 Million Campaign for money."[12] Gross wanted the Convention to appoint a central committee, with L. R. Scarborough as chairman, to organize a nationwide program of evangelism. Since the 75 Million Campaign was still active, however, the Convention wisely declined to establish a new national committee for this purpose. Instead, state conventions, associations, and local churches were encouraged to begin their own evangelistic programs, with aid and leadership from the Home Mission Board.[13] The board's Department of Evangelism was already proving itself very capable in its task and was the natural choice for such an endeavor.

"Our evangelists have had a great year," the Home Mission Board reported.[14] Credit was given to the 75 Million Campaign for the success of Southern Baptist missions in America. The Campaign had allowed the average Southern Baptist to participate in the work of the denomination, and as a result interest levels in missions and evangelism grew proportionately. South-

Giving a New Direction 85

ern Baptists were simply more interested in their denomination than they ever had been. The New Denominationalism which grew out of the Campaign had a direct corollary in the heightened interest in evangelism. "The outlook is glorious," said the board.[15]

Scarborough also highlighted the new evangelistic spirit at the 1921 meeting. In his report on the Conservation Commission he called attention to the perception among Southern Baptists that evangelism was more important than before.

> The tides of spiritual and evangelistic and missionary power which have swept over our churches, bringing hundreds of thousands into the fold, the mighty vision which He has given to our people, the establishment of the sacrificial and heroic spirit, the deepening of the prayer life of our churches, the calling out of more than 10,000 of our young people in the spirit of voluntary service to give their lives to Him, the development of a great denominational consciousness, the development of a new and stronger leadership among our people, ... puts us under everlasting obligation to our God and under a new sense of a responsibility to go forward in a new, greater fashion. The question is whether or not we will be big enough for our day, to see our opportunities and enter the open doors that God is offering to us.[16]

Scarborough hoped that Southern Baptists would fulfill what he considered their foremost destiny — to evangelize the whole world. It was a destiny that required the very best in leadership and strategy.

CALLING OUT THE CALLED

While Scarborough was fully committed to a program of personal evangelism, he gave equal attention to enlisting young Christians for full-time vocational ministry. He believed that focusing on young people who might feel an urge to pursue a career in the church served as a multiplying agent in overall evangelism. He termed this effort "Calling Out the Called"[17] and mentioned it regularly in both lecture and writing.

In his first book, *Recruits for World Conquests*, published in 1914, Scarborough devoted an entire chapter to the subject of encouraging youth to accept Christ's call to the ministry. He saw both human and divine aspects in an individual's choice to enter Christian service. "God calls," said Scarborough, "and man calls out."[18] But, for Scarborough, it was not just a single human delegate that served as envoy of the divine call. Instead, a plurality of persons entered into the equation of influence: parents, teachers, pastors, evangelists, and missionaries all played a part in issuing the human side of God's call.[19] By recruiting even one person for vocational ministry, the effects of the Gospel were multiplied and the work of the Southern Baptist Convention continued.

Scarborough looked to Christ himself as the model of this kind of enlistment. He thought of Jesus as the founder of the "first school of evangelism" and saw in him the unification of both the divine and human factors of the call.[20] On one hand, Christ called disciples to follow in his ministry; on the other, he "called out" certain ones for special tasks in evangelism. It was these few, Scarborough believed, who truly understood the methods espoused by Christ:

> This inner compulsion of a divinely transmitted missionary passion at once drove each disciple out after the next one in his circle, whether in the home, in society, or in business. If each disciple of Christ in all the world would act on that divine impulse germinating in regeneration and foster that passion and feed it and give it a chance to express itself, the whole world would be brought to Christ in a generation.[21]

The multiplication of disciple upon disciple in this method was indispensable to Scarborough's view of world evangelism. He saw the possibility of a never-ending circle of "Calling Out the Called," where the ones summoned by the divine call also included a plea for vocational ministry in their own messages.

It was a primary purpose of Baptist colleges, Scarborough felt, to aid in leading young Christians into the ministry.[22] While he acknowledged the value of education in other fields, such as law or medicine, he believed the main objective of Baptist academia was to provide a "trained, Christian leadership."[23] Scarborough visualized a great mass of graduates returning to local churches to take leading roles in evangelistic programs. These young leaders would become the driving force of the next generation of Southern Baptists and indeed the conscience of

Giving a New Direction 87

the denomination. Without this "trained, Christian leadership," Scarborough saw no future for the New Denominationalism.

In the same way, Scarborough pointed to the seminaries as important training centers for evangelism.[24] Of course, he hoped that those called into the ministry would enter a Southern Baptist seminary for doctrinal and denominational instruction. A vital part of "Calling Out the Called" was moving them toward a sound theological education. For Scarborough, however, a seminary curriculum was incomplete without a thorough emphasis on evangelism.[25] The institutions themselves must infuse the students with an evangelistic spirit that resulted in both personal evangelism and a commitment to call young people into the ministry.

One means of insuring an evangelistic curriculum in seminaries, Scarborough maintained, was for all institutions to follow the lead of Southwestern and establish a full professorship in evangelism.[26] Classes in evangelistic methods, wrote Scarborough, "should be required of all students in the ministry . . . and taught by a teacher noted for his compassion for a lost world and his power in leading men to Christ."[27] In addition, books with evangelistic themes—like those written by Scarborough himself—formed the foundation of a comprehensive theological education.[28] Scarborough believed that this kind of education was the logical outcome of calling young Christians to vocational service.

The evangelistic emphases in seminaries were not an end in themselves. Scarborough pictured a vast army of denominationalists returning to local churches with a vision of reaching the world for the Southern Baptist Convention. An evangelistic curriculum would give the Convention the kind of leaders needed to thrust the denomination forward. As Scarborough envisioned:

> [They] would furnish our churches, mission boards, and mission fields, and a lost, destitute world with a *living* ministry and would cause Christ's Kingdom to come in all lands by leaps and bounds. A soul-winning pastor in every church, soul-winning teachers in every Sunday School, soul-winning editors in every religious paper, soul-winning deacons, . . . soul-winning young people's leadership, would soon take this world for Christ and His truth. We cannot do it by evangelists alone. We must have evangelistic pastors, teachers, deacons, and soul-winning women in our churches if we are to take the world for Christ.[29]

Scarborough saw a contagious effect in evangelism. Those called into the ministry, and properly trained at evangelistic seminaries, carried the desire back to the local field where others were inoculated with a yearning for personal evangelism.[30] In this way, the cause of Christ and the growth of Southern Baptists were coupled so that both benefited.

In the end, "Calling Out the Called" was a failed endeavor if the person lacked the "evangelistic spirit."[31] For Scarborough, one's heart had to be set on winning converts to Christianity. The spirit of evangelism was to pervade everything a minister of the Gospel said and all aspects of his work. Scarborough had a clear picture of those ministers:

> They will know that men who do not believe are lost, condemned, under the wrath of God, hell deserving, hell going, breakers of God's law, crucifiers of Christ, sinners without hope and without God in the world, dead in trespasses and sins, and with a kindred compassionate love, which melted the heart of a dying Saviour, they will extend loving arms and helping hands, tender hearts every way to these lost sinners.[32]

In Scarborough's opinion, the fate of the lost was so evident that the demand for an effective evangelistic force was a natural deduction.[33] Those who were called into the ministry must make evangelism a primary concentration for their entire careers.

Scarborough was convinced of the necessity of evangelism courses in Baptist colleges and seminaries.[34] He was personally committed to teaching classes which emphasized the theory and practice of evangelism and retained his professorship until retirement. He saw in these classes the opportunity to transfer to students his own evangelistic zeal and at the same time strengthen Southern Baptist evangelism as a whole—which further established the New Denominationalism.

EVANGELISTIC TEACHING IN THE CLASSROOM

The importance placed on evangelism courses at Southwestern Seminary was unmatched at any other academic institution. From the beginning, Scarborough laid out a curriculum that covered two full years of study.[35] The course work of the first

Giving a New Direction 89

term emphasized personal evangelism, while the second year focused on evangelism practiced by a local church. Scarborough designed these classes as two hours of lecture per week and a rather extensive reading schedule.[36]

When B. H. Carroll first planned to start a department of evangelism in his Seminary, he intended for it to have an "inside and an outside phase."[37] The inside phase was, of course, the "Chair of Fire," with L. R. Scarborough as Southwestern's model evangelist. The outside phase was an ambition to place a number of evangelists in the field as representatives of the Seminary. This latter phase was realized for a time during Scarborough's tenure as president.[38] However, Scarborough's focus remained on the evangelism classes and involving every student in a thorough study of evangelistic method.

In the main, Scarborough's lectures were based on expositions of Scripture. He dealt a good deal with the role of the Holy Spirit in evangelism and used passages from the book of Acts to support his thesis.[39] From Acts, chapter thirteen, for example, Scarborough showed how the church in Antioch chose Paul and Barnabas for a special mission. For Scarborough, this episode formed the basis for "Calling Out the Called."[40] Once again he pointed to a divine motive with a human expression. The Holy Spirit, said Scarborough, was the source of every evangelistic enterprise, yet he preferred to act through human institutions like a local church.[41]

Scarborough taught that the Holy Spirit began "church evangelism" on the day of Pentecost described in the second chapter of Acts.[42] In so doing, God had given the standard for this kind of evangelistic activity. Just as the leader of the Jerusalem church — the Apostle Peter — was at the forefront of this early revival meeting, the pastor of the local church, Scarborough believed, should lead in the church's evangelism. He was not discounting the value of professional evangelists, but sincerely felt that the "main work of evangelism" was each pastor's responsibility.[43]

For Scarborough, no real evangelism was possible without the power brought to it by the Holy Spirit. It was his divine activity which initiated both the desire for evangelism and the method for accomplishing this sacred work.[44] The Holy Spirit was not only the originator of an evangelistic venture, according to Scarborough, but it was necessary for him to take personal interest in every facet of the operation:

> The Holy Spirit's presence and power are absolutely essential to revivalism — the winning of one or the winning of multitudes. There is no substitute for the Holy Spirit's power, and if there is no Holy Spirit there is no Pentecost. Any effort without Him is futile and fruitless. He is the one essential.[45]

Scarborough never taught that there was no need for human intervention. He saw the results of human activity in the Scripture and in his own experience. Still, he held firmly to the conviction that divine action was preeminent if a church was to fully accomplish its task in evangelism.

A MODEL FOR EVANGELISM

In Scarborough's assessment, the foremost evangelist of all history was the Apostle Paul.[46] This first-century evangelist possessed a "four-fold vision," said Scarborough, which made him a prototype for all evangelists.[47] First, Paul realized his own sinfulness. Second, he was satisfied that the Gospel itself had the power to save him. The Apostle's third vision was of Christ as the one who was uniquely able to act as Savior. Finally, he saw that the world was in need of his message of hope. Paul had a "holy courage," Scarborough declared, which equipped him with a faith and optimism unknown by most believers.[48]

The central action of evangelism, in Scarborough's opinion, was the preaching moment. In this, too, he looked to the Apostle Paul as the model for evangelistic preaching.[49] While Scarborough did not think that Paul was necessarily the most accomplished orator that ever stood in a pulpit, he believed that the Apostle's preaching had a power that was unmatched.[50] It was a power that enabled Paul to persuade a nonbeliever and bring him into the Christian community. Above all, though, the directness of Paul's preaching brought results with every proclamation. Scarborough was most impressed with the frank theme of a Pauline sermon: "It was evangelistic, always. It won."[51]

Paul was somewhat of an enigma to Scarborough. He recognized and admired Paul's intellectual ability, yet was more enthralled with the simplicity of his method. On the one hand, the Apostle was a "spiritual philosopher,"[52] but on the other he was "bold, plain and always simple."[53] Scarborough saw in Paul an example of how evangelists were to go about their jobs. Paul displayed an adeptness for blending with his surroundings, and modern evangelists were to emulate his flexibility.[54] In Scarborough's mind, one could do no better than to mimic the Apostle at every move.

THE NEW TESTAMENT AND EVANGELISM

While the study of other doctrines was important, Scarborough held steadfastly to the belief that evangelism was the principal teaching of the New Testament.[55] In the Gospel accounts, the book of Acts, and the Pauline writings, Scarborough was able to find evangelistic motifs on almost every line. Even before the ministry of Christ he perceived an evangelistic strain in the Gospels. "The message of John the Baptist," Scarborough wrote, "was a soul-winning message."[56] Still, he looked to Christ as the inventor of the methods of evangelism in the New Testament.

One of Christ's chief functions, in Scarborough's view, was his role as "Messianic evangelist."[57] From the beginning of his ministry to his ascension, Christ was mainly concerned with enlisting disciples. In the very words of the Great Commission (Matthew 28:18-20), Scarborough saw five principles which related to an evangelistic program. Christ's command to go into "all the world" was the basis of the "extensive principle."[58] Scarborough interpreted these words to mean that a local church was to reach out to the entire community, regardless of social class. In addition, this principle was supportive of taking a census of the community and compiling a list of prospects. The second, "intensive principle," was drawn from the urgency of taking the Gospel message to "every creature."[59] An individually based personal evangelism was called for by these words.

Scarborough's third and fourth principles came from the idea of baptizing and teaching new Christians. The principles of "obedience" and "sanctification" were the foundation of training programs for new church members.[60] Finally, the "principle of personal companionship" was derived from Christ's promise to always remain with his disciples. The believer's attention was to be continually fixed on the person of Christ, because his presence gave victory in evangelistic activity.[61]

Evangelists were not only to obey Christ's commands but also to follow his example. To the very end the Savior was concentrating on evangelism. Even in the crucifixion, Scarborough recognized the evangelistic spirit when Christ "stopped dying to save the penitent sinner."[62] It was in Christ's command "Follow me" and in his example of personal evangelism that Scarborough discovered the true motives for Christian witness.

In Scarborough's judgment, the New Testament was filled with patterns for evangelism. From the Apostle Peter's "Model Evangelistic Sermon" in Acts, chapter two, to the standards given by Paul in Galatians, a system for evangelism was available for every Christian.[63]

> The New Testament message is God's evangel. The heaving heart of compassion beats in every nerve center of New Testament truth and sends the warm pulsating blood of soul-winning from the very heart of Christ. The preacher, the teacher, the Sunday School and young people's organization, the women, the laymen, whatever be the individual or group working in Christ's kingdom, who does not see that compassionate evangelism is the supreme matter in the New Testament had read the Book with closed or short-sighted vision.[64]

The portraits of Christ and the Apostles offered ideals for every personal evangelist. For Scarborough, though, it was the New Testament itself which provided the requisite authority for every believer to share his witness for Christ.

STRATEGIES FOR EVANGELISM

The revival meeting, in Scarborough's estimation, was the main forum for churchwide evangelism.[65] He thought every church should have an organized plan of preparation for revival. Although the individual preacher chosen and the messages delivered were important, Scarborough felt revivals must be founded on prayer and a system of reaching persons in need of Christ.[66] In the same way, said Scarborough, while leaders must be sure to give the church a desire to make contact with non-Christians, they must not overlook details such as advertising the meeting.[67]

Beyond the local church, however, Scarborough called for an "institutional" evangelism.[68] Southern Baptists were to look to denominational agencies for an overarching vision for evangelistic campaigns. The mission boards, Scarborough thought, could teach the entire Convention effective methods for evangelism: "They form rallying centers, centers of spiritual power, out from which goes the strength of a great people."[69] The Foreign Mission Board and Home Mission Board together raised a unified voice for Southern Baptists. Denominational institutions, then, enabled Baptists to put forth a broader program with a consolidated message. For Scarborough, the evangelism of the New Denominationalism hinged on the willingness of the Convention to unite under the banner supplied by its institutions.

Southern Baptists were not to rely solely on national agencies, however, to accomplish the work of evangelism. Scarborough taught that churches and individual believers had an equal share in shaping evangelistic methods.[70] In addition to revivals in local churches, Scarborough insisted on "mass evangelism" that included both indoor and outdoor meetings.[71] Further, personal evangelism was not to be considered a secondary task. Instead, advised Scarborough, "Southern Baptists should more and more pursue, seek and do their utmost to win men and women of all ages and kinds to Jesus Christ personally."[72]

When churches and individuals placed proper importance on evangelism, Scarborough believed, they became more productive tools for Christ's cause:

> Nothing is more powerful than an evangelistic church. It will do more for a community, lift and build more hearts and characters, and save more souls, and raise more money, and generate more spiritual movements for civic, domestic, social and political richness in a community's life. It will make a church conquering. It will make the ministry invincible and give them a grip on humanity and God that the devil will find hard to break. It will make giants out of pigmies [sic] in the ministry. All the power Christ has, and He has it all, is guaranteed to the individual or the group of individuals who are mastered by this mighty passion to go make disciples . . . .[73]

The methods of evangelism produced practical results. Scarborough insisted that not only individual lives would be enriched, but the whole community would experience renewal because of a church's evangelistic program.

Scarborough also counseled his students to plan a follow-up program for revival meetings. New church members and new Christians should be invited to classes especially designed for their needs.[74] "It is not enough to *save souls*," Scarborough proclaimed. "We should also seek to *save lives* for the service of God."[75] Scarborough taught his student-pastors to take the lead in continuing the spirit of evangelism in their churches.[76] In Scarborough's understanding, revival preparation, organization, and follow-up were equally important parts of successful evangelism.

GOAL OF EVANGELISM

In the final analysis, Scarborough's teaching on evangelism was more than methods and strategies. He was ultimately concerned with people joining the Christian community. He believed that evangelism called for a passion that fully consumed the minds of every church and every church member.[77] Once Southern Baptists committed their total energies to reaching the world for Christ, it would be only a matter of time before the Gospel message circled the globe. "Our supreme challenge," Scarborough declared, "is massing, mobilizing, utilizing our millions."[78] His students were numbered among the millions of Southern Baptists, and Scarborough realized that the evangelistic outreach of the New Denominationalism depended upon their abilities and willingness to serve.

EVANGELISTIC THEMES IN WRITING

L. R. Scarborough was a prolific writer. In addition to dozens of pamphlets and hundreds of articles, he published sixteen books during his career. One of the duties B. H. Carroll prescribed for his professor of evangelism was to produce literature that could be used in evangelistic training by Southwestern Seminary.[79] It was soon discovered, however, that the entire denomination was clamoring for this kind of instruction. Scarborough's books carried his spirit of evangelism beyond Seminary Hill and helped shape the evangelistic methods of a great many Southern Baptists.

Scarborough used two of his works as the texts for his classes in evangelism. The first, *With Christ After the Lost*, published in 1919, became his most enduring book and comprised the first year of study for evangelism students.[80] The second year of study was based upon *Endued to Win*, which Scarborough published in 1922. While Scarborough focused on the ministry of Christ in the former book, he used the latter to reveal strategies for evangelism practiced by other leaders of the New Testament Church.

Comprising five units, *With Christ After the Lost* takes methods used by Christ and the Apostles and applies them to modern denominational structure. Some topics, like evangelism on the day of Pentecost[81] or the examples laid out by the Apostle Paul,[82] echo Scarborough's class lectures. The book is formatted to accommodate a systematic study of evangelism in every area of ministry.

In Part I, "Some Spiritual Prerequisites," Scarborough centers on the individual soul-winner. Of course, every evangelist must have had a personal experience of salvation.[83] In addition, though, the faith and commitment to evangelism expressed by the soul-winner is to be of such a pristine nature that there can be no question about his devotion to the task. "Winning one creates the hunger for more," Scarborough explained, "and on it goes till a consuming spiritual passion burns in every corpuscle of our being to win others to Jesus Christ."[84]

Scarborough searched the New Testament for model evangelists, such as John the Baptist and Jesus Christ himself, for Part II, "Some Inspiring Examples." It is in the third unit, "The Way to Win," however, that Scarborough brings the foundational principles of evangelism into the modern church. Deacons, pastors, and Sunday school teachers are targeted for special instruction. Church programs like revivals and doctrinal studies are also singled out as places to emphasize evangelism. It is a "Constructive Evangelism" that Scarborough hopes his readers will adopt.

Scarborough was always concerned that evangelistic practice be rooted in New Testament doctrine. "Christ's order" was the foundation stone that evangelistic methods must never displace:

Christ's New Testament program for souls is salvation, confession, baptism, church membership, instruction, service. We cannot break nor disregard Christ's order and grow a permanent, constructive evangelism. . . . The New Testament is largely made up of instruction in character, culture and aggressive service.[85]

In "Personal Work," Scarborough's fourth unit, he shows how methods are best used to reach the unsaved on an individual basis. He begins with "Suggestions to Winners,"[86] where he points out essentials to personal witness. The most important ingredient, in Scarborough's opinion, is prayer. "It is absolutely necessary that you keep in and up with God," he wrote.[87] An intimacy with Scripture and a patient attitude complete Scarborough's profile of a successful soul-winner.

Part V, "Scripture Passages for Workers," links Bible verses together into a narrative of God's promises for the evangelist. Scarborough's own words of advice are interspersed with various portions of Scripture to compose a quick reference tool in the practice of evangelism. For instance, verses from Romans, Galatians, and Psalms are followed by Scarborough's exhortation that by "right of ownership Christ is entitled to our best service."[88] This unit allows the reader a closer look at Scarborough as he shares some of his favorite Bible verses.

Scarborough's second evangelism textbook, *Endued to Win*, follows a similar format to the first. In this book, written three years after the first, in 1922, one is able to compare points of emphasis as the author reinterprets evangelistic technique for the more advanced reader. Preaching, prayer, and revivalism are again pronounced the keys to successful evangelism. This second text, however, particularly stresses the activity of the Holy Spirit in calling individuals to the Christian faith.

Divided into three "books," *Endued to Win* devotes a full third of its space to the work of the Holy Spirit. Through fourteen chapters Scarborough outlines how the Spirit provides the local church and its members with power:

> The Holy Spirit is given by the Father as pilot and guide of the souls and activities of Christ's people in their search for truth and in their quest for souls. . . . He throws His lambent light both on the page of revealed truth and on the heart of the

Giving a New Direction 97

saved soul, matching the supply of the one to the need of the other. He goes before [the] world's need, calls the worker, selects the part of the vineyard of the Lord He desires each to labor in.[89]

For Scarborough, the Holy Spirit leads the church in its evangelistic programs. Spiritual energy provides each evangelist with both the call to the task and the means to accomplish this special service.

In the final section Scarborough again returns to the model evangelistic tactics of such notables as Paul, Peter, and Barnabas. The preaching of Paul and the leadership of Peter make each of them prime examples of the kinds of evangelists Christ wants in his ministry. Barnabas was a "great church builder," Scarborough said, and is worthy of emulation.[90] Interestingly, the author also includes a chapter on "Soul-Winning Women." He singles out Elizabeth, John the Baptist's mother, and the "four Marys" for particular honor and proclaims that each of these women "made a contribution of great value to the life and service of Gospel leaders."[91]

Scarborough's second text remains closer to the New Testament era than *With Christ After the Lost*. While both books apply biblical principles to modern denominational activity, *Endued to Win* stays firmly planted in the evangelistic endeavors of the first-century church. In both of these works, Scarborough insists that evangelism is the supreme function of Christian people. As individual believers connect with the spiritual power available through prayer and study of the Scripture, a mighty evangelistic force is created to carry Christ's message of hope and salvation. Through these two evangelism textbooks, then, Scarborough was able to convince his students of the primacy of evangelism in the New Testament and the power of personal witness in the New Denominationalism.

PERSONAL EVANGELISM

The witness of individual Christians formed a recurring thesis in all of Scarborough's writing. Although he placed great worth in the evangelistic programs of local churches, the personal soul-winner was for Scarborough the champion of Christendom. He never lost sight of his own responsibility to herald the Gospel message and challenged his readers to accept the same obligation.[92]

Scarborough turned once again to the call of Christ for his authority in personal evangelism. "Christ means for all groups of disciples . . . to be soul-winners," Scarborough declared.[93] He insisted that the stress on evangelism was not a product of his own ingenuity, but a result of Christ himself exacting from every Christian a pledge to carry his message. Scarborough was convinced that Jesus Christ places in every believer an "inner compulsion" to share his witness.[94] This inward touch of the divine conscience drives each Christian to become active in evangelism.

All committed evangelists, in Scarborough's view, hold common characteristics. The prerequisite experience of personal salvation is followed by a behavioral change which produces a Christ-like character.[95] Loyalty to Christ, a desire to convert non-Christians, and familiarity with the Bible comprise some of the other elements that soul-winners have in common. These traits come to the forefront as believers are transformed into evangelists. In the end, these personal evangelists arrive at the same certainty.

> A deep conviction of the sinner's need, a spiritual apprehension that men, women and children out of Christ are now already lost, unsaved, alien from God, conceived and born in sin, hopeless, Christless, Godless, under the wrath of God, condemned already, and without Christ speeding towards eternal night.[96]

It is this conviction, Scarborough explained, that pushes these soul-winners to reach large numbers of people with the Gospel.

As far as Scarborough was concerned, no real evangelism could occur without a prominent place given to prayer. "God's people must pray for the power of God," he wrote.[97] Nothing was an effective substitute for the power of prayer in Scarborough's understanding of the way evangelism worked. "Prayer," Scarborough felt, "is an absolute essential."[98]

While the spiritual power available through divine contact was crucial, Scarborough returned again and again to the human factor in personal evangelism.[99] The Holy Spirit, he said, is certainly active in the process of calling persons to Christ—indeed,

Giving a New Direction

he is the initiator—but this fact does not release individual Christians from their duty to tell of an obtainable salvation. God chooses to use his Spirit in evangelism, but he also employs church members in his message of hope:

> He not only calls through His providences, but through His people, as well. I will tell you one of the chief values of the Christian life today, in mother, or father, or child, or preacher is the value that it has in the testimony to call people to the Lord Jesus Christ. Your life and mine is the embodiment of God's speaking at the door of the heart of the unsaved.[100]

For Scarborough, the personal evangelist symbolized the heart of the Gospel message. It was an individual Christian reaching out to an individual unbeliever that most completely portrayed the love and grace of Christ.

CHURCH EVANGELISM

The witness shared by individuals was only one-half of the evangelistic strategy recommended by Scarborough. He was equally committed to an evangelism expressed through the programs and corporate outreach of a local church. Special services for evangelism, revivals, worship services, and Sunday school were all appropriate avenues for calling the unsaved to the Christian faith.[101]

The preaching moment constituted, in Scarborough's mind, the peak of church evangelism. The preacher was "God's man in the pulpit" and the message he proclaimed was of the utmost significance.[102] Preaching was not entertainment, but an announcement of God's plan for humanity.

> [It has a] holy purpose, blood-soaked, tear-stained purpose to win from sin, ignorance and death, and to build up in the heart the highest ideals of the gospel. A spiritual consciousness of the issues, eternal destinies involved in the souls and imperiled lives whose very eternity is at stake.[103]

While the teaching program of the church was not to be neglected, Scarborough was persuaded that it was in preaching that the true work of church evangelism was done.

Scarborough taught that it was possible to intentionally build an evangelistic church.[104] Since evangelism was Christ's main intention for the church,[105] it was his desire for Christian leaders to design churches centered on evangelism. Scarborough defined the components necessary for such a church. In addition to a devoted pastor, the church needed leadership committed to evangelism, as well as the support of the entire congregation. Every program of the church had to be aimed at winning converts; even the types of hymns sung, Scarborough contended, could help create an evangelistic atmosphere.[106] Intentional choices by the church and its leadership were the cause of the spirit of evangelism permeating every program sponsored by a given congregation.

Christians had been anointed as ambassadors of Christ and his Kingdom, Scarborough concluded.[107] It was the responsibility of church members to participate in the primary mission of every congregation. The "evangelization of the spiritual life of man" was God's command to his followers.[108] As Scarborough contemplated the evangelistic program of the church, he visualized the positive effect on individuals and the community. Just as a personal witness strengthened the life of a believer, church evangelism empowered the denomination to endure into the next generation.

SUMMARY

L. R. Scarborough was uniquely suited to teach Southern Baptists about evangelism. As professor of evangelism for Southwestern Seminary he directly influenced the attitudes of thousands of students. As general director of the 75 Million Campaign he organized a mass crusade in both evangelism and enlistment to Christian service. Finally, as an author, Scarborough chose evangelistic themes almost every time he took pen in hand. Quite simply, evangelism was the driving force of Scarborough's personality.

By the early twentieth century, Southern Baptists were ready for a renewed emphasis in evangelism. As early as 1906, messengers to the Southern Baptist Convention expressed a desire to more fully organize evangelistic efforts. As a result of a movement led by B. H. Carroll, the Home Mission Board was instructed to establish a department of evangelism. By the time Scarborough appeared on the national scene, steps had already been taken to insure the continuation of the denominational message.

It was not Scarborough, then, who instigated the new thrust in evangelism. The tide of evangelistic fervor began to rise as a precursor to his involvement. Instead, Scarborough was swept up by this new movement when he joined the faculty of Southwestern Seminary. Within a few months of his appointment, however, he was already exhibiting his trademark zeal for evangelistic endeavor. From an unassuming beginning as a member of the panel of evangelists at Hot Springs, Arkansas, in 1908, Scarborough quickly moved to a leadership role in the evangelistic program of Southern Baptists. He did not create the initial movement, but by 1920 he was at the forefront of a new level of intensity in evangelism. By then Scarborough was well on his way to making evangelism a vital part of the New Denominationalism.

While Scarborough may not have been a technical scholar,[109] he did possess a zest for the written word. In sixteen books, written over a period of twenty-eight years, Scarborough proclaimed his messages of evangelism and denominationalism. Again and again he wrote of the reasons for building evangelistic churches and instilling the evangelistic spirit in every Christian. However, it was not a general evangelism that he championed. Rather, it was a decidedly *Southern Baptist* evangelism. The evangelistic programs that Scarborough promoted were forever linked with the agencies, schools, and churches supported by Southern Baptists. He not only hoped to convince an unbeliever to convert to Christianity, but to join a Southern Baptist church.

The message that Scarborough sent to his students and readers was that evangelism was central to New Testament faith. It was a message that permeated every book and every classroom lecture, and in time the man and the message became one and the same. Scarborough was convinced that without a substantial program in evangelism the Southern Baptist Convention would not endure as a major contributor to the Christian cause. For him, evangelistic zeal was the guarantee of the New Denominationalism.

CHAPTER 5

Thinking Through It All

Lee Rutland Scarborough died on April 10, 1945, at the age of seventy-four.[1] He was buried in Fort Worth. During a career that bridged two centuries and spanned six decades, Scarborough touched the denomination of Southern Baptists at almost every level. From the local church to Southwestern Seminary; from the pastorate to the Convention presidency; and from the pulpit to the written word, L. R. Scarborough voiced the resounding themes of Southern Baptist life. He was first and foremost a Southern Baptist, and this denominational identification colored both his work and his personality.

The "Chair of Fire," later renamed the L. R. Scarborough Chair of Evangelism, gave Scarborough his first exposure to national acclaim. As professor of evangelism at Southwestern Seminary, he was entitled to speak to Southern Baptists about the primary concerns of the denomination. Soon, however, he broadened his message to include the hope for a New Denominationalism within the Convention.

ANALYSIS OF A DENOMINATIONALIST

W. W. Barnes, an early church historian of Southwestern Seminary, wrote that devotion to the denomination was an "ob-

Scarborough and wife, c. 1940.

session" for Scarborough.[2] All else became secondary as Scarborough's intense loyalty increased with the progression of his career. Even while serving as a pastor, he tended to place the concerns of the denomination above those of his local congregation. Biographer H. E. Dana said that it was Scarborough's "policy as a pastor to press the great missionary and denominational causes."[3] The success of the denomination became an all-encompassing goal for Scarborough's ministry.

The radical denominationalism of L. R. Scarborough was not purely a product of his own invention. To be sure, he seemed especially adept at focusing a great deal of energy on the Southern Baptist mission. Still, like everyone, he was shaped into the person he became by the experiences of family, culture, and the age in which he lived. For example, if Scarborough's parents had been members of a Methodist church, or if he had attended a Lutheran college, then the philosophies which attached themselves to his mind would have been of a different nature. Would Scarborough have become a Southern Baptist leader if his father had practiced law and encouraged him to pursue a legal career as he originally intended? If Scarborough had never met B. H.

Carroll, would the annals of Baptist history even record his name? The particular influences that came into his life helped to mold Scarborough into a loyal *Southern Baptist* denominationalist.

Southern Baptists are greatly indebted to Scarborough's parents for the results of his career. George W. Scarborough was a bivocational Baptist preacher. Although the responsibilities of running a West Texas ranch were never-ending, the elder Scarborough managed to tour neighboring towns and settlements regularly to preach the Baptist doctrines of faith, grace, and salvation. Martha Rutland Scarborough was a conscientious mother who constantly reinforced the Baptist identity of her home. The Scarboroughs saved for years to build a new house, but decided to use the money to send young Lee to Baylor University. In Mrs. Scarborough's mind, nothing but a Baptist college would accomplish the kind of education she desired for her son. A Baptist home and a Baptist education instilled in L. R. Scarborough an irrevocable identification with the denomination of Southern Baptists.

In addition, George W. Scarborough extracted from his son a promise to hear B. H. Carroll preach every Sunday while he was in Baylor University. It was in the First Baptist Church of Waco that Scarborough received his theological education. Under the booming voice and logical arguments of Carroll, the tenets of the Christian faith began to take permanent form in Scarborough's understanding. While Baylor provided a liberal arts education, it was B. H. Carroll who gave Scarborough a theology.

Although he graduated from Baylor still looking toward a career in law, Scarborough was unable to detach himself from the denominational call. While studying at Yale University, he could hear the voices of his mother and father asking him to consider a life in the ministry. Carroll's sermons played again and again in his mind until finally the urge within his spirit was overwhelming and he yielded to the divine call to preach the Gospel. It was not just any Gospel that he would preach, however. It would be the same Baptist message he had learned in home, school, and church.

While he was successful in the pastorate, the fullest expression of Scarborough's denominationalism can be found in his years at Southwestern Seminary. From the very beginning B. H.

Southwestern faculty dinner, c. 1935.

Carroll looked to Scarborough as second-in-command: He chose the location for the Seminary, coordinated the fund-raising project to develop the property, and supervised the erection of the first building. Soon, though, Scarborough was elevated from Carroll's primary assistant to heir-apparent. Carroll virtually handed the presidency of Southwestern to Scarborough and expected him to continue building a denominational institution. Carroll's intentions were not thwarted.

Scarborough was not content with Southwestern remaining the sole property of Texas Baptists. He wanted the entire Southern Baptist Convention involved in the Seminary's growth and development. From the first, he was convinced that Southwestern would become a world-class academic institution. With that purpose in mind, Scarborough persuaded the Seminary trustees to transfer ownership of Southwestern to the Convention. He was determined to lead a *denominational* Seminary and took every step necessary to insure the participation of all Southern Baptists in his academic enterprise.

At every turn Scarborough gave the denomination preeminence. He took a leave of absence from Southwestern to organize the 75 Million Campaign. He served as president of both the Baptist General Convention of Texas and the Southern Baptist Convention. He represented his denomination in the Baptist World Alliance. Scarborough defended the denomination and its institutions against the attacks of J. Frank Norris. During a ministry of almost fifty years, Scarborough never put local interests before those of the denomination. He was, indeed, an obsessed denominationalist.

It may be impossible to calculate all of the results of his obsession. While some are easy to tally, such as the continued existence of Southwestern Seminary, others are more intangible. How does one quantify the impact of Scarborough's denominational devotion on individual lives? The direct influence on his students and the indirect effect through their ministries continue to produce results. In the same way, it is difficult to total the consequence of Scarborough's denominationalism on the Southern Baptist Convention. The fallout of the 75 Million Campaign can be settled, but the infusion of his denominational spirit into the institutions and programs of Southern Baptists is not so easily determined.

Perhaps it is enough to say that in his role as a denominationalist Scarborough helped Southern Baptists to achieve greater potential. His legacy includes the world's largest free-standing theological seminary, a better organized Convention structure, and a stronger Southern Baptist identity through the *Baptist Faith and Message*. By his untiring efforts on behalf of Southern Baptists, L. R. Scarborough gave a new definition to "denominationalist" in this century.

EVALUATION OF THE NEW DENOMINATIONALISM

Scarborough was aware that the 75 Million Campaign created a New Denominationalism for the Southern Baptist Convention. Interestingly, he may not have understood the central role he played in fashioning the new Convention structure. Certainly he realized the organization he gave to the Campaign, but he seemed to overlook his more important contribution. In short, Scarborough infused the Campaign with vision. It was a vision of a more cooperative Convention; a more global Convention; and a more denominationally minded Convention.

The word "cooperation" became synonymous with the name "Scarborough." He spoke and wrote constantly of the concept of Southern Baptist cooperation. For Scarborough, to be a true Baptist was to be a cooperating Christian. He did not want local churches to relinquish autonomy by any means. In fact, he initially opposed the 75 Million Campaign because he perceived a threat to the independence of individual congregations. When he saw the power available in such unity, however, he gave his full strength to making the Campaign a success.

From the beginning, Scarborough hoped the Campaign would produce more than money. In addition to the increased cooperation that was a natural by-product of the program, Scarborough longed for the Campaign to enlarge the hearts of Southern Baptists for evangelism. He believed the 75 Million Campaign would have been an utter failure had only the monetary goal been reached. Instead, he wanted unbelievers to join the fellowship of Christianity and young believers to join the ranks of vocational ministry. His program for evangelism centered on "Calling Out the Called" and he reached for the multiplication factor of disciple-to-disciple enlistment.

The cooperation and evangelistic thrust that reverberated from the Campaign produced the principle of a New Denominationalism within the Convention. In 1921 the Department of Evangelism of the Home Mission Board expanded its efforts to reach the unsaved. By the end of the 75 Million Campaign in 1925, Southern Baptists were committed to continuing the unified program. The Cooperative Program—the most visible expression of the New Denominationalism—was a direct consequence of the Campaign. By lending his expertise in management and fund-raising to the 75 Million Campaign, Scarborough spear-headed an intense New Denominationalism that altered the organizational structure of the Southern Baptist Convention.

Scarborough's evangelistic teaching and writing were equally important components of the New Denominationalism. In his opinion, the whole of Christian theology could be summed up in the practice of evangelism. His books were not scholarly, theoretical treatises. Rather, they were practical manuals of how evangelism worked in the New Testament and how biblical principles could be applied to Christian witness in the twentieth century. If given the choice between the pragmatic and the academic, Scarborough would choose the former every time. He invested his students not merely with scholarship but with the practical means of accomplishing the evangelistic task. Scarborough's method did not produce scholars but "soul-winners." The New Denominationalism, then, had more to do with propagation than theology.

By the mid-1920s, Southern Baptists wanted to reach the entire world with the Gospel message. The 75 Million Campaign had proven that they were capable of gathering the financial support necessary for such a venture. The Cooperative Program gave them the ongoing organization that could carry out a global program. Congregations across the Convention were more concerned with the unified efforts of the denomination than they ever had been. For the first time in Southern Baptist history, local churches placed the interests of the denomination above their individual agendas and the New Denominationalism took precedence over factional concerns.

For Scarborough, the New Denominationalism was distinctively Baptist. While he was willing to reach beyond the boundary of the Convention to embrace the Baptist World Alliance, his vision for Southern Baptists did not incorporate an inter-denominational ecumenism. The programs, institutions, and causes he devoted his life to supporting were all uniquely Baptist in nature. Scarborough's focus was always on increasing the potential of the Southern Baptist Convention. Indeed, he believed Southern Baptists were uncommonly suited for realizing the Great Commission. When he hoped for a New Denominationalism to emerge from the 75 Million Campaign, it was so that Southern Baptists might become more intensely loyal to the missionary and evangelistic endeavors that he was persuaded only they could achieve.

As a result of the emphasis on unified programs in the early 1920s, the passionate display of denominationalism that characterized L. R. Scarborough was exhibited throughout the entire Convention. A renewed devotion to all things Southern Baptist became the hallmark of local churches, associations, and state conventions. In the end, the New Denominationalism gave the Southern Baptist Convention the impetus to forge a larger place for itself in the Christian community. It was a force that helped denominational institutions survive an economic depression and a second world war. At the same time, the New Denominationalism sealed the Southern Baptist identity on church members and new converts alike.

Perhaps those kinds of effects are too much to expect from the work of one person. However, when the individual in question is L. R. Scarborough, the New Denominationalism seems to be a logical outcome. It may be too soon to evaluate the full ramifications of the New Denominationalism, but Scarborough's leadership in the movement is a certainty. Indeed, we are unsure of whether the New Denominationalism is still in force. The fundamental changes both within the Southern Baptist Convention and American society as a whole in the past twenty years have in some ways left the idea of denominationalism behind. Many people are now more interested in individual causes than in the unified work of a denomination. We may have to wait a few more years to gain the proper perspective on the overall impact of Scarborough's ideology.

We must always use discretion in determining the causes of large shifts in the historical landscape. Still, the connection of Lee Rutland Scarborough with the New Denominationalism carries with it the proof of solid historical data. When all has been said, Scarborough's New Denominationalism had a positive impact on the programs and people that constituted the Southern Baptist Convention after World War II. It remains to be seen what sort of *new* New Denominationalism will emerge in the next century.

APPENDIX A

Lee Rutland Scarborough: A Chronology

1870   Born July 4 – Colfax, Louisiana
1892   Graduated Baylor University (B.A.)
1896   Graduated Yale University (B.A.)
        Accepted pastorate in Cameron, Texas
1899   Entered Southern Baptist Theological Seminary
1900   Returned to Cameron Baptist Church
        Married Mary P. (Neppie) Warren
1901   Accepted pastorate of First Baptist Church – Abilene, Texas
1908   Became first professor of evangelism for Southwestern Baptist Theological Seminary
1915   Inaugurated as second president of Southwestern Baptist Theological Seminary
1919   Named general director of Baptist 75 Million Campaign
1920   Elected chairman of 75 Million Campaign Conservation Commission
1925   Transferred ownership of Southwestern Seminary from Baptist General Convention of Texas to Southern Baptist Convention
1929   Elected president of Baptist General Convention of Texas
1938   Elected to first term as president of Southern Baptist Convention
1940   Named vice-president of Baptist World Alliance
1942   Retired from public service
1945   Died April 10 – Buried in Fort Worth, Texas

APPENDIX B

Scarborough's Statement of Faith

In the late 1920s, Scarborough was asked to write a statement of his beliefs. Apparently, there was some question about his doctrinal stand on particular issues. This may have been in connection with his controversy with J. Frank Norris. (See the *L. R. Scarborough Collection*, File 10.) Scarborough's statement follows:

First—I believe most heartily all the fundamentals of the faith set out clearly in the famous articles of faith called the "New Hampshire Articles of Faith" believed by Baptists the world over. I think this is one of the clearest statements of the content of God's word on the fundamentals of the gospel.

Second—Particularly, I would say that I believe in the absolute diety [sic] and perfect humanity of Jesus Christ. He is absolute God in the perfection of man.

Third—I accept without equivocation, his holy life, his virgin birth, his atoning death on the cross, as God's substitute for wicked men and that by his shed blood men are saved and saved only by him. I believe in his bodily resurrection and his personal visible return some glorious day.

Fourth — I believe the Bible – old and new testament — divinely inspired, errously [sic] perfect in its doctrine; flawless in its standards of righteousness. God's inbreathed and infallably [sic] inspired will to men. My dear preacher father taught me the verbal inspiration of the Bible. Dr. Carrol*[sic]*, in his teachings confirmed the teachings of my father and all my studies since have not changed my views on this great subject. I believe that it is a vital book given us by the breath of the divine spirit as God's will and doctrine and practice; I love it as such; I teach it as such; I preach it and am trying to live it as such.

Fifth — If there is one stran *[sic]* or streak of modernism in the veins of my theological faith, I do not know it. I am a conservative in my theology. I reject and repudiate the whole theory of evolution as God's method of making man and the world. I believe that according to Genesis, God created, not evoluted man. I repudiate the results and correlative of the modernistic, evolutionary idea of man's creation. I am a simple old-time Baptist in all these matters. I have never endorsed or encouraged modernism nor evolution. I have never made any contacts or commendations nor endorsements of the modernistic theory which has embarrassed my simple faith nor the friends of the gospel of such belief. That I have thus endorsed these things is made out of the whole cloth of falsification.

Sixth — I am a cooperative, constructive Baptist. I believe in Missions from my own redeemed soul clear out to the last lost man to the utmost parts of the world. I believe in Christian education, our schools and colleges and Seminary, and the leaders of these institutions. I believe in christian *[sic]* hospitals, orphanages and all other of these healing and helping institutions. I believe Christ gave us a three-fold program following his example from my own redeemed soul out to the last lost man. In this place by preaching a crucified Christ as the only remedy for sin for all men and this world-wide evangelism and in training the minds of men by christian *[sic]* education in christian *[sic]* schools and Seminaries, carry out the will of Christ. I believe that all the teachers in these schools should be orthodox and sound in the faith and when they cease to thus teach, they ought to cease their connections with these schools, and third, I believe in hospitals and orphanages, all those benevolent institutions or enterprises that help to heal the diseases of the bodies of man. This is Christ's redemptive program. I believe in consistent, faithful storehouse tithing, not as a matter of legalism, but as a matter of obedience and grace. I believe in offerings beyond the tithe and I believe that Christ's method of giving the tithe is the weekly budget, thus turn the tithe into the treasury of the church and there to be distributed to all causes, Missions, Education and Benevolences.

Seventh — I also believe that preachers and others ought to tell the truth. I believe that you can be orthodox on the doctrine of our faith and heretical on the practice of it. A preacher who deliberately, for selfish ends, lies and misrepresents a brother or an institution, puts himself in the category of heretics, modernists and evolutionists. Certain widely published statements about my administrationsand *[sic]* the affairs of the Seminary have greatly misrepresented my administration. I wish to say that the Seminary books and money are handled by two bonded good men and are audited by registered auditors and are examined by the Board of Trustees of the Seminary, composed of twenty-five as good men as Southern Baptist Convention are able to find. All my administrative acts are guided and reviewed by these twenty-five good men and a full report and detailed statement of all transactions is reported annually to the Southern Baptist Convention and any constructive, truth loving Baptist may have access to my books any day. We have destructionists from the beginning of God's Kingdom; we will have them to the end; it seems to be a part of the Devil, to block God's Kingdom. The thing for the constructive, right-thinking people of God to do is to go on constructively, cooperatively like Nehemiah did, and build the wall and let the destructionists go on to their certain doom of isolation and desolation.

If this plain statement of facts will help the cause of Christ, or the Baptists in the West or anywhere else, I am happy to make it.

APPENDIX C

Letter from J. Frank Norris

J. Frank Norris was pastor of the First Baptist Church of Fort Worth, Texas, when Southwestern Seminary was established. In fact, Norris served on its board of trustees in the early years. With a mixture of both theological and personal differences, Norris and Scarborough carried on a public and private dispute for well over a decade. The following letter from Norris, written on October 28, 1924, from the Hotel Bender in Houston, was a typical exchange. While no direct reply from Scarborough can be found, he responded many times in like manner. For an example see Appendix D. (This letter is from the *Scarborough Collection*, File 261.)

My dear Dr. Scarborough:

I have just read with a great deal of amusement, mingled with pity, your latest attack on me published in the "Baylor Lariat" and I understand published in two other local papers.

First of all if there are any further favors you and those of like mind as yourself can render me by giving me larger audiences and a wider hearing, I confess that I should express to you my profound appreciation. It is deeply regretted however that you send out your tracts and special publications at the expense of the mission money of the denomination, which thing you have been doing now for the last three years.

You are making yourself a laughing-stock of even your closest friends.

When Dr. Brooks [Baylor University president] broke faith with the denomination and came out and defended evolution in the Baylor Bulletin in December, 1923, just one month after he had stated that he was "opposed to evolution of every phase and kind," you told him he had made a collossal *[sic]* blunder. Why don't you now stand up to your report that went to the Tarrant County Association, in which you opposed and repudiated the stand of Dr. Brooks and his associates? What are you afraid of? It was pathetic the way you hedged, straddled and compromised to Dr. Brooks when he went after you immediately after he received my telegram concerning the action of the Tarrant County Association.

Are you opposed to evolution or are you in favor of it?

Do you still hold the view in your letter to Dr. G. W. McPherson in which you advocated evolution? I have never yet published this letter, only made incidental reference to it? *[sic]*

Your bitter attacks on me have not gotten you anywhere, but on the contrary they have cost you very heavily. You take brethren into confidence and tell them things that are untrue concerning me and these brethren sit right down and write me or tell me about them.

For instance, you unloaded all the bitterness of your soul to Dr. C. M. Thompson of Kentucky when he was with you a short time ago. Dr. Thompson did not do a thing but go back to Kentucky and tell some friends of mine that you were the craziest man he ever saw, and expressed his profound pity for you in your bitter attitude toward me.

Why you have lost your judgment and don't exercise your ordinary common sense and see the "handwriting on the wall." *[sic]*

The Baptist Standard and directors turned you down, have turned you down repeatedly; on an article following the Galveston Convention in which you made a bitter attack on me. Several of the directors told me about it and you had to admit it a short time ago.

You carried a bitter attack down to the Star Telegram [Fort Worth newspaper] on me and they refused to publish it, even for pay. Even the nondescript, irresponsible Tribune said your article was libelous and they had to eliminate portions of it it *[sic]* that was so bitter. *[sic]*

Your own faculty are divided against you and your policy and they have told you so.

I am just mentioning these things so you may know that I know of your course.

I not only have no bitterness for you, but I have come to have a profound pity for you.

Appendices 117

You have used everything at your command to injure me, and you have only added to me instead of hurting me.

You lost your temper and blamed me for the discussion concerning your famous "land deal" when you secured a large block of land in connection with the location of the Seminary. I was not the cause of the discussion. The deed records of Tarrant County speak for themselves. A few months ago an auditor, the one who has been auditing the books, in the main for the Baptists of Texas for several years came over from Dallas and checked over this record — I did not have him do it — but certain leading Baptists in Dallas were interested in it.

I have never accused you of any wrongdoing — it was others who criticized you for taking half of your offering that you raised at a certain City in Texas, instead of sending the entire amount in to the headquarters at Dallas. I am not saying anything about it. The records speak for themselves, and the brethren in Dallas have done the talking.

You lost your temper when it was discussed, and continued to be discussed, the fact that you changed the auditor's report of the Seminary. I was not the one that told it. The records speak for themselves.

It was nothing short of amusing how you were willing to enter into a dark, foul blackmailing scheme against me. The other parties who were asked to go into it say that you were the main instigator. They have given me all the facts concerning it.

I greatly admire the work you have done, but brethren everywhere wonder whether you have a monopoly on the personal pronoun "I."

You came down here to Houston just before my meeting began and did all you could to hinder it, and now we are having the greatest campaign in the history of Houston. Already more than 400 have joined the church. The church has been benefitted and a new day has come. this *[sic]* is not counting the benefits to other churches. We had a $10,000 budget expense for the Tabernacle, lot, and other expenses, and we are just a little more than half through, and lack only $1600 being paid out.

Therefore, if you can do anything to help me in my next meeting in a similar way, I shall appreciate it. There are quite a number of the best places in Texas that are urging me to come.

For instance, I am going to Arlington in Tarrant County, the largest and best place in the County outside of Fort Worth.

They are going to have a large tent or tabernacle. The meeting will be held next spring. I shall appreciate all that you may do similar to your fine work here in Houston.

I need not go further; I am just writing you a letter which you are at liberty to publish at any time and at any place you may see fit.

I notice in your article statement to the effect that I am building a great paper and a powerful Church, or words to that effect. You are eminently correct. Plans are now about finished to let a contract for additional improvements, more room and more buildings, which will be let immediately upon my return from Houston.

You dear brethren who have so utterly lost your heads have rendered me as great a favor as the envious brethren of Joseph rendered him. Only a few days ago a great magazine with 2,800,000 circulation sent a member of the staff to write up the full history of me and my work.

It is rather significant that simultaneous with your ardent proposition that your "hat was in the ring" and you were going to put the First Baptist Church and its pastor out of business— I repeat it is rather significant that simultaneous with your threat against me because I exposed evolution, that I should suddenly be given a hearing at the world's greatest pulpits. Excuse me, Dr. Scarborough, for seeming to boast, but I am sure you are generous enough to rejoice in the success and promotion of another. So you have rendered a great service in many ways.

There is a scripture which I think of a great deal that fits the case: Philippians, 1:12,

> "But I would that ye should understand, brethren,
> that the things which happened unto me have fallen
> out rather unto the furtherance of the gospel."

I notice where you indicate or threaten that my seat is going to be challenged at the coming convention in Dallas. In order that you may be thoroughly informed I here now announce that I am going as a messenger of the First Baptist Church, and I challenge you to make your challenge!

Be assured, Dr. Scarborough, I have written you in the finest vein of humor and I quite sympathize with you in the awful predicament that you and others find yourselves. Everybody has laughed at your predicament from start to finish.

For instance you joined in with me in putting Dr. Rice, a

Methodist infidel, out of a Methodist University three years ago, but when I turned my guns on Baptist infidelity then you turn your guns on me. That has been the hugest joke in the whole drama.

Be assured I wish you the very best and greatest possible success and do rejoice and shall rejoice for every soul that is won under your ministry. When you and I get to Heaven, which I am sure the abounding grace of God is sufficient to take care of us both, we will have many good times sitting down and talking all these matters over.

APPENDIX D

The Fruits of Norrisism

Sometime in the late 1920s, Scarborough wrote and distributed a small tract which he titled "The Fruits of Norrisism." By the time of its publication Scarborough was convinced that J. Frank Norris stood for everything which he himself stood against. Scarborough believed that Norris and his ideology should not be allowed to go unchallenged, and he wrote about it with a directness that reveals several years of conflict and frustration. (See the *Scarborough Collection*, File 652.)

FOREWORD

This tract is a discussion of some of the fruits of an old cult under a new name. The following are some of the characteristics of this cult — Norrisism:

1. It is toward true religion what socialism and bolshevism are to politics and industry wholly destructive in spirit and methods.

2. It is anti-missionary and anti-institutional. It gives nothing to associational, state or home missions and only enough to foreign missions to get representation in the convention. It spends most of its money on itself — some times in court trials for perjury, arson and murder, and in sending out free literature seeking to destroy the causes other people try to build.

3. It thrives on sensationalism, misrepresentation and false accusations of good men and true causes. It masquerades under the cloak of anti-evolutionism, anti-modernism, anti-catholicism in order to ride into public favor and cast poisonous suspicion on the leadership of the causes of constructive Christianity.

Appendices

4. In its chief leadership it is the embodiment of autocratic ecclesiasticism. All the privileges and rights of the church heading up in the pastor.

5. It uses the public, the press, and the radio to create suspicion, to foment class prejudices and to vent its hatred against innocent personalities and institutions.

6. It divides and splits families, churches, associations and strikes its poisonous fangs at the brotherhood of Christianity.

7. It lowers the standards of right conduct, individual righteousness, ministerial ethics, personal integrity, and gives to the world a false conception of the character, spirit and methods of Christianity.

8. The only people or causes it praises are those who bow down to its dictum or fail in any wise to cross its path.

9. The individual, the preacher or church who joins in sympathy with this cult will sooner or later cease to co-operate with the mission, educational or benevolent enterprises fostered by God's people.

10. It has some noble names upon the escutcheon of its false accusations and public misrepresentation; Carroll, Gambrell, McDaniel, McConnell, Mullins, C. V. Edwards, Brooks, Sampey, Groner, Ray, Robertson, Forrest Smith, Cullen Thomas, Truett and others — multitudes of false accusations, such as: infidelity, graft, heresy, theft and such like, and groundless insinuations have gone out against these good men for years. This tract deals with only a few of these false and slanderous charges against these brethren. These are but samples — there are many others which are as groundless as these.

Since wide publicity has been given in other ways to the recent action of the Tarrant County Association, it is felt that the matter should be accurately set out in the columns of the Baptist press in Texas.

It is generally known that the Tarrant County Association has been the storm-center of a ceaseless and vicious attack upon the boards, institutions, causes and leaders of Texas and Southern Baptists for many years. It began in the days when B. H. Carroll first moved to Fort Worth and has gone on, night and day, with increasing momentum until today. The same source of confusion in Baptist affairs has carried on agitation in every other phase of life in Fort Worth — political, commercial and social. It has been a bitter, ceaseless turmoil for many years. Almost all officers and prominent men in every line of life have been under fire. It has been in the courts, as trials for perjury, arson and murder will show. It is remarkable how Tarrant County Baptists have stood up for the truth and stood for all the Baptist causes and stood together. Baptist ministers' conferences have again and again repudiated this presumptuous leadership by expulsion. The Tarrant County Association has denied it fellowship by large and increasing majority. The Baptist General Convention, for three successive years, by practically unanimous vote, refused it membership in its councils. This action was taken by these various bodies because patience has ceased to be a virtue in dealing with the persistent, pestiferous, and reckless misrepresentation of the sacred causes to which the denomination is dedicated.

This same old fight was brought up again in this Association and was disposed of in a manner which ought to make a deep impression on right-thinking people everywhere. One of the smaller churches, led by its pastor, some days before the associational meeting, sent a letter containing certain criticisms of the institutions and leaders of the Baptist causes in Texas and certain grounds on which they desired seats for its messengers in the Association. This letter was sent to the clerk of the association and others. After the letter had been read and the pastor of the church given abundant time to present his views, the association promptly with but little discussion on the part of the members of the association, by a vote of 208 to 14, refused seats to the messengers of this church. Also, a young brother reputed to be not yet out of his teens, and who was recently licensed to preach under the same destructive opposition, presented a widely advertised set of resolutions demanding that this association request the President and Faculty of Baylor University to sign the McDaniel resolution passed at the Houston Southern Baptist Convention. Some brother in the association objected to the consideration of these resolutions and the vote was promptly taken, and the young brother was refused a hearing by unanimous vote. In this way in just a little while, in a fine Christian spirit, both of these attacks on the causes from the same old source, were repudiated by the association.

There are involved in this action of the association *[sic]*.

SOME GREAT PRINCIPLES

1. The principles of co-operation. The church above alluded to in its letter stated, after quoting the Commission in Matt. 28:18–20, "Therefore, we are not in sympathy with the unscriptural institutionalism which has no place or authority in the Great Commission." The constitution of the Tarrant County Association in Article II says, "The object of this association shall be to establish a means of communication between the churches, to project measures for the furtherance of the cause of Christ within its bounds, and to promote among the churches the support of all the general denominational, missionary, educational and benevolent enterprises." That is, the Association's main object is to promote and support the mission boards, schools, hospitals, orphanages and other enterprises and institutions founded by our fathers and which are supported by the Texas General Convention and the Southern Baptist Convention. The pastor and his church in question stated, in accord with the teachings of this old source of trouble in Tarrant County, that they have no sympathy for nor cooperation with these institutions. In other words the association stands for those causes and institutions and the church in question does not.

The other ground on which they were refused seats as stated by the resolution, was: the action by the pastor and the church in question, clearly showing that he and the church were willing to become a part and parcel of a guerilla [sic] warfare which for years has plagued the denomination.

The Tarrant County Association clearly recognizes the privilege of this church to refuse cooperation in building our mission causes, our schools, seminaries, hospitals and orphanages, but it denies them the right to come into fellowship of an association which is in favor of all these things and yet at the same time tries to decide the Association's course in supporting these institutions. The resolution of non-co-operation passed by this church was found to be in complete accord with their non-support of these causes. Their letter stated that they had given nothing this last year to Home Missions, Foreign Missions, State Missions, Assuciational Missions, Christian Education, Seminaries, Orphanages, Hospitals, and so on. All this clearly shows that they did not want to co-operate, but to dictate and to keep others from doing what was right for these causes, during the last many years. Isn't it strange that a pastor and a church, that announce both in theory and in practice, that they are opposed to the things you are trying to do, want fellowship with you and seats in your councils for the sole purpose of trying to keep you from doing the things you want to do? This does not look like New Testament co-operation to me.

2. The Principle of Loyalty to the Commands of the Lord

Jesus Christ and the Causes and Institutions which these Commands and Teachings Set Up and Set Forward.

This pastor and church state clearly, both in theory and in practice, their opposition to the institutionalism of the Commission. He in his argument, the pastor, tried to establish an alibi, by saying that he meant unscriptural "institutions," such as institutions that teach evolution, and so on. But he unfortunately used "unscriptural institutionalism." Now he and the self-assumed leadership which he is following are opposed to institutionalism of Southern Baptists. Their gifts this year, or their lack of gifts, state that this institutionalism which they are opposed to is missions of all sorts, education of all sorts, and benevolences of all sorts. Their action in not giving speaks as loud as their profession on non-co-operation. The brotherhood had just as well know that the leadership of the opposition in Texas and the South is not only opposed to some of the institutions that are dear to us, but it is opposed to the principle involved in their establishment and promotion. That leadership gives practically nothing to any of the causes and institutions fostered by Texas and Southern Baptists. It is pure, downright anti-mission, hardshellism, and anti-institutionalism. Wherever that leadership gets a hold on individuals or churches they at once cease to give to the great causes of the Commission. Try it out in any community and you will find it so. This is a leadership of non-co-operation, anti-missionary and destructive, and is a leadership of death to all who follow it. It has been from the beginning when it made a bitter, cruel fight on B. H. Carroll seventeen or eighteen years ago, kept it up on J. B. Gambrell, and has kept it up continuously on nearly every leader Texas and Southern Baptists have had to this day. It is construction against destruction. It is the old fight known all through the ages. Its principle method is misrepresentation, inuendo [sic], suspicion, accusation against character and leadership. It does nothing for the causes itself, but seeks to keep others from doing what they want to do for the causes.

3. The third principle involved in this matter is loyalty to the moral laws of God.

God says, "Thou shalt not bear false witness against they [sic] neighbor." The main basis of this notorious opposition is a palpable violation of this plain commandment of God. This opposition to the causes of Tarrant County Association, and Texas Baptist and Southern Baptist Conventions has ceaselessly misrepresented their causes, therefore, the Tarrant County Baptist Association puts itself, again, with overwhelming force and with a solidarity and a conviction that rings to Heaven, against this opposition and its misrepresentations. It is not only a question of veracity, honor and common honesty in denominational relationship. I itemize some cases:

(1) This opposition has published widely that I said "Prof. Meroney and the Medical College at Dallas must go." I never said that nor anything that could be twisted into such a statement.

ABOUT DR. BARNES

(2) It also published that Dr. W. W. Barnes, Professor of Church History in the Southwestern Seminary, is an evolutionist. There is not a syllable of truth in this statement. In 1921, when this agitation first began, I asked Dr. Barnes to write out a statement of his faith and submit to me. His statement was passed around among the faculty of the Seminary. Each one of them voluntarily signed it, and here is what Dr. Barnes says: "We repudiate the rationalistic method of dealing with the Bible and religious truth that has come into vogue in Europe and in many universities and seminaries in our own country in recent years, and the results thereof. We repudiate the evolutionary theory that man has come by a process of development from any lower animal. We believe that he is the direct creation of God, both on the physical and mental or spiritual sides of his being. We believe in the Genesis account of the origin of the world and of man. We believe that it is the only true and satisfactory account of the origin of the world and of man to be found in any literature."

Then he goes on to affirm his belief in the fundamentals — the inspiration of the Bible, the deity of Christ, and so on. There can not be found one scintilla of evidence, in the fourteen or fifteen years of teaching of this fine teacher in the Southwestern Seminary, where he gave the slightest coloring of belief in the evolutionary theory. The faculty of the Southwestern Seminary is an absolute unit on, and have unanimously by standing vote endorsed the McDaniel resolution, and this reflection on Dr. Barnes is untrue.

ABOUT JUDGE GORMLEY

(3) This same source of opposition has published and broadcasted that Judge J. W. Gormley, lecturer on Medical Jourisprudence [sic] in Baylor Medical College, is a Catholic.

Hon. Cullen F. Thomas and Dr. F. M. McConnell, two honorable and truthful men who are in possession of the facts, say that this accusation is untrue. Hon. Charles O'Connell, present President of Dallas Bar Association, corroborates this statement, and Judge Gormley himself says that he has had no connection with the Catholics church for sixteen years. Furthermore, Judge Gormley is a Mason, and Masons are not Catholics. God says, "Thou shalt not bear false witness against they [sic] neighbor."

FURTHER ABOUT JUDGE GORMLEY

(4) I charge a yet graver offense against upright dealing among men and fair play by this same self-appointed censor of faithful servants of our Baptist institutions. Through published word and by radio it spread throughout the land the sensational scoop that Judge J. W. Gormley, cultured scholar and modest gentleman, on Sunday afternoon, 4:10 o'clock, July 30, in the city of Dallas, on McKinney Avenue, was caught by officers in a raid of a notorious gambling house and promptly pleaded guilty and paid his fine, under an assumed name.

This charge was absolutely untrue. It was no more true of John W. Gormley than of John Calvin or John Knox, or John Wesley or John Bunyan.

I here and now announce upon incontestable proof, that not only was this reckless, cruel charge against a good man's good name not so, but that the one who gleefully rolled the unfounded story as a sweet morcel [sic] under his tongue, knows his statement was not so.

ABOUT CULLEN F. THOMAS

(5) Another item of conscienceless misrepresentation and untrue purport is the charges out of this same source of misinformation [sic] as broadcasted and published concerning Hon. Cullen F. Thomas, deacon of the First Baptist Church, Dallas, and one of the most honorable and useful laymen among Southern Baptists. These charges are that he has asked large and exorbitant fees for legal services in connection with the Relief and Annuity Board, Baylor Medical College and other institutions, securing loans for these enterprises. These charges are utterly untrue and baseless. The facts are that Mr. Thomas has rendered valuable legal service requiring much time and expense, in the interests of the Executive Board, of

the Texas Convention, The Relief and Annuity Board, Baylor University, with the institutions at Dallas and Waco, the Southwestern Seminary, the Baptist Standard, Baylor College, Howard Payne College, and others. For most of these services he has received no fees at all, and in the cases where he has received fees they have been small and modest, and in every case paid at the instance and instigation of the institution themselves. Why should this good man be thus falsely charged? God says, "Thou shalt not bear false witness against thy neighbor."

ABOUT PROF. MERONEY

(6) This same source of opposition brings now Prof. Meroney, a teacher in the field of science in Baylor University, under cruel and relentless fire. His only ground of attack is quotations from a book which Prof. Meroney is using in his classes. Prof. Meroney himself says, on the same page on which the damaging quotation is given, the following:

"In order to get before the beginning students something of the meaning of the folk ways, more and institutions as conceived by Mr. Sumner, a number of extracts are here given, by permission of the publishers." There follows the quotation from Prof. Sumner's book. Prof. Meroney says that the words used by Prof. Sumner are not his words, and he does not endorse them. But Prof. Meroney said on October 1924 and endorses that statement today, as follows: "I do not believe nor teach that man was evolved from lower forms of life. On the other hand, I do believe that man came into existence by the direct creative act of God, as stated in Genesis 2:27." I have talked in the last few days to a number of graduates of Baylor University, all honorable, cultured, truthful, sensible men and women, who took Prof. Meroney's studies in science, and they unitedly say that Prof. Meroney not only does not believe in the evolutionary theory, but clearly sets out the reasons why he does not. God says, "Thou shalt not bear false witness against thy neighbor."

ABOUT DR. BROOKS

(7) This same source of opposition says that Baylor University faculty and President Brooks are against the McDaniel Resolution passed by the Southern Baptist Convention, and ought to be made to sign it.

I want to say, in the first place, that the McDaniel Resolution was the Southern Baptist Convention's request to the institutions and boards owned and controlled by the Southern Baptist Convention, and that resolution did not ask individual signature to the McDaniel Resolution. It said, signify their approval of that resolution. The Southwestern faculty, by unanimous vote standing, endorsed the McDaniel Resolution. The Southwestern Seminary is owned by the Southern Baptist Convention; and all other boards and institutions of Southern Convention ownership have signified their approval of the McDaniel Resolution. Baylor University is not owned by the Southern Convention, and the Convention did not ask, and the resolutions do not require, that the state institutions subscribe to resolutions passed by the Southern Baptist Convention.

I wish to say further, that President Brooks was present and voted for the McDaniel Resolution and published his endorsement, and further as everybody knows, the faculty of Baylor University has already passed, voluntarily and unanimously, a signed expression of their belief in the fundamentals of our faith, which articles of faith wholly endorsed in principle the McDaniel Resolution. Now, why is it necessary, when President Brooks voted for the Resolution and the faculty had already endorsed that principle and all the other fundamentals of faith by their personal signature, why nag and raise suspicions and untrue charges against a great set of honorable, consecrated, orthodox teachers?

The Tarrant County Baptist Association, with a unanimous and thundering vote, said to this opposition, "We will have no part in further criticism or misrepresentation or inuendo or insinuation against President Brooks and his noble faculty." God says, "Thou shalt not bear false witness against they [sic] neighbor."

ABOUT DR. McCONNELL

(8) It has been charged time and time again that Dr. F. M. McConnell, former Secretary of Missions in Texas and in Oklahoma, noble pastor, College President, successful evangelist, suddenly left Oklahoma because when his books were opened there were suspicious things found therein. There is not the slightest truth in this charge. It is baseless and pernicious. No truer or nobler man walks the earth than F. M. McConnell.

Appendices 129

ABOUT DR. GRONER

(9) Dr. F. S. Groner, successful pastor with a great reputation as a Secretary and leader of Texas Baptists, stainless in soul with an unimpeachable character, has been charged with the closed policy, with malfeasance, and other high crimes in connection with certain printing matters and the use of denominational position to domineer the dictatorially control denominational affairs, the misappropriation of funds and other things.

Investigations have been made concerning these charges and this noble secretary has been elected unanimously by a widely-scattered and honorable set of men composing the Texas Executive Board for ten years. Every charge brought against him has been subject to the clear light of investigation and proven false and yet these charges are repeated and the attempted assassination of this good man's character has gone on in wide broadcasting and publication. God says, "Thou shalt not bear false witness against thy neighbor."

The records of Dr. Groner's ten years of faithful service in denominational achievement will compare favorably with that of any other State Secretary in the yorld *[sic]* — living or dead. His character is unimpeachable.

ABOUT DR. CAREY

(10) Recently E. H. Carey, Dean of Baylor Medical College, noble Christian gentleman, addressed a group of Baylor students in Fort Worth. He talked on the growth of the Baylor Medical College from a small obscure medical school in an insignificant building up to the great standard "A" college with magnificent buildings and faculty and student body as it is now. And after speaking of this wonderful growth he said, "This is a form of evolution that I believe in, that Dr. Brooks believes in, and we all believe in." Yet this statement was twisted and turned to a bare statement that Dr. Carey and Dr. Brooks were evolutionists with reference to the creation of man. This sort of falsifying is pernicious and ought to be frowned upon by right-thinking men everywhere.

ABOUT SUPT. DURHAM

(11) This same leadership of this old cult anti-mission, anti-institutional recently made a bitter personal attack upon the character of the Superintendent of the Baptist Hospital of

Fort Worth, bringing libelous charges and cruel insinuations against this good man's character — A man who is clean in his private life, noble in his services to God and humanity. These efforts to malign men, to assassinate their characters on false charges, baseless and groundless, is a part and parcel of its fight against hospitals, mission boards and educational institutions, masquerading under the name of fundamentalism.

ABOUT GAMBRELL AND TRUETT

(12) This destructive cult and some deceived by its false statements have circulated the report in pulpit, press and over radio as is quoted in a charge recently made by a deacon of a Baptist church, who is under the dominance of Norrisism as follows: "The big trouble is that Drs. Brooks, Truett, Gambrell, Scarborough, Groner and others had misappropriated a considerable amount of the funds of the 75 Million Campaign." The facts are as everybody connected with the 75 Million Campaign knows or can know that these men handled only the money sent to them by the State Secretaries or the church treasurers for their individual causes, and that the treasurers of these institutions are under bond and have their books audited by registered auditors every year and that no charges by the auditors or friends of these causes have ever been lodged against any of these men. The only money of the 75 Million Campaign that Dr. Gambrell ever saw was that part of his pledge he paid before he died and he died early in the campaign. Is it not a shame that such men as Gambrell, Truett, Groner and Brooks should be thus publicly held up as thieves and scoundrels. These school men and secretaries accused of all these crimes have every year been unanimously elected to their positions and have never been charged with arson, perjury or murder.

I was charged with misappropriating $100,000.00 of the Seminary money because I charged off to "profit and loss" worthless endowment notes to the amount of more than $100,000.00. Not one cent of interest or principal had been paid on any of these notes for ten or more years. I had been carrying these notes as assets and under the advice of my auditor I charged them to "profit and loss." I still have these notes in the safe of the Seminary and would be very glad to collect those two that are signed by the chief opposer of these causes with nothing paid on them for fourteen years.

ABOUT WHAT GOD HATES

(13) If Norrisism misrepresents and brings false accusations against such causes and men, masquerading under a cloak of orthodoxy and fundamentalism, can such a cult be trusted in anything? Can one afford to believe its reports of its own membership; the size of its own congregations; the additions it has, the numbers it has in Sunday school and glaring sensational reports of the greatest revivals in the world? An investigation of the facts back of these swelling numbers will more than likely find them greatly exaggerated. God says in His word "Six things doth the Lord hate—a proud look, a lying tongue, hands that have shed innocent blood, a heart that deviseth wicked imaginations, feet that be swift in running to mischief and false witness that speaketh lies and he that soweth discord among brethren."

Will it profit a man if he is sound in his theology on creation according to Gen. 2:27 and yet violates God's command where he says, "Thou shalt not bear false witness against thy neighbor." Ex. 20:17.

TARRANT COUNTY ASSOCIATION GOES ON GLORIOUSLY

(14) We believe that the brotherhood everywhere ought to come out strongly and stand for and speak for and support these causes, institutions and these leaders who are sound in the faith and are giving themselves and their money, sacrificially, to the building of these institutions and causes, which this age-long fight of anti-missions, anti-leadership is fostering to ruin the causes and work of Jesus Christ. The Tarrant County Association has spoken time and time again. We live close to and know the method, the spirit, the character and life of this opposition. The Tarrant County Association is humbly grateful to God that; though we are closest to this long, ceaseless attack on our causes, yet we are united, with practically every preacher, pastor and church in the Association standing full-length for the causes, giving last year nearly $100,000.00 to the denominational causes outside of our bounds and baptizing nearly 1,200 new converts into the fellowship of our churches. We are united for the things of Christ and His old truth, and solidly against those who oppose these causes and His truth.

We are against evolution, modernism, and also lying. We have never shielded nor protected evolutionists, nor are willing to protect those who falsely accused the true leaders of Christ's causes.

It will be charged that this tract is paid for out of Mission Money. That will be as false as the other charges made by Norrisism against good men and causes.

This tract can be secured in considerable numbers by application to its author, Seminary Hill, Texas.

Notes

INTRODUCTION

1. L. R. Scarborough, *Recruits for World Conquests* (New York: Fleming H. Revell Co., 1914).
2. L. R. Scarborough, *Marvels of Divine Leadership, or the Story of the Southern Baptist 75 Million Campaign* (Nashville: Sunday School Board Southern Baptist Convention, 1920), 63.
3. H. E. Dana, *Lee Rutland Scarborough: A Life of Service* (Nashville: Broadman Press, 1942).
4. L. R. Scarborough, *Prepare to Meet God* (New York: George H. Doran Co., 1922).
5. L. R. Scarborough, *Holy Places and Precious Promises* (New York: George H. Doran Co., 1924).
6. L. R. Scarborough, *A Modern School of the Prophets* (Nashville: Broadman Press, 1939).

CHAPTER 1

1. George W. Scarborough Bible, L. R. Scarborough Collection, 13, Archives, A. Webb Roberts Library, Southwestern Baptist Theological Seminary, Fort Worth, Texas. The Scarborough Collection consists of over five linear feet and 870 files. It is a comprehensive collection of letters, articles, manuscripts, speeches, official documents, and photographs. Henceforth items will be referenced according to their individual forms and followed by "SC" (for Scarborough Collection) and the file number.

H. E. Dana, *Lee Rutland Scarborough: A Life of Service* (Nashville: Broadman Press, 1942), 15, calls Scarborough's mother "Martha Elizabeth." While the family Bible only lists the marriage of "Geo. W. Scarborough to M. E. Rutland," Dr. Scarborough in his manuscript "The Evolution of a Cowboy," SC, 17, gives his mother's name as "Mary Elizabeth Rutland." For clarity she is henceforth referred to as Martha.

2. L. R. Scarborough, "The Evolution of a Cowboy," 1, SC, 17.
3. Scarborough Bible, SC, 13.
4. *Ibid.*
5. Unpublished Manuscript, SC, 24.
6. Scarborough, "The Evolution of a Cowboy," 1, SC, 17.
7. Scarborough Bible, SC, 13.
8. Confederate Army Billing Statement, SC, 15.
9. Dana, 15. Much of the material in Dana was given to him directly by Scarborough and can be considered as more than just a secondary source.

10. Scarborough Bible, SC, 13.
11. Scarborough, "The Evolution of a Cowboy," 22, SC, 17.
12. *Ibid.*
13. *Ibid.*
14. Unpublished Manuscript, SC, 24.
15. Dana, 27.
16. *Ibid.;* Cf. Scarborough, "The Evolution of a Cowboy," 2, SC, 17.
17. Scarborough, "The Evolution of a Cowboy," 2, SC, 17.
18. Unpublished Manuscript, SC, 24.
19. Dana, 19.
20. Scarborough, "The Evolution of a Cowboy," 15-16, SC, 17.
21. *Ibid.,* 2.
22. *Ibid.*
23. Dana, 25.
24. Quoted in Dana, 25-26.
25. Scarborough, "About My Call to Preach," SC, 1.
26. *Ibid.*
27. Scarborough quoted in Dana, 21.
28. Scarborough, "The Evolution of a Cowboy," 5, SC, 17.
29. Quoted in Dana, 23.
30. Scarborough, "The Evolution of a Cowboy," 22, SC, 17.
31. Charles T. Ball, "The House That Was Never Built," SC, 4.
32. Scarborough, "The Evolution of a Cowboy," 22, SC, 17.
33. Scarborough quoted in Dana, 26.
34. Unpublished Manuscript, SC, 24.
35. L. R. Scarborough to J. B. Cranfill, 14 June 1927. SC, 28.
36. *Ibid.*
37. Scarborough, "The Evolution of a Cowboy," 8, SC, 17.
38. *Ibid.,* 9.
39. *Ibid.*
40. *Ibid.*
41. Scarborough to Cranfill, SC, 28.
42. *Ibid.*
43. Scarborough, "The Evolution of a Cowboy," 11, SC, 17.
44. Dana, 36.
45. Scarborough, "The Evolution of a Cowboy," 7, SC, 17.
46. *Ibid.,* 10.
47. Dana, 36.
48. Scarborough, "The Evolution of a Cowboy," 13, SC, 17.
49. *Ibid.*
50. *Ibid.*
51. Dana, 38-39.
52. Scarborough, "The Evolution of a Cowboy," 17, SC, 17.
53. *Ibid.*
54. Dana, 39, adds an interesting footnote to this story. Thirty years later Judge Leggett was present for Scarborough's inauguration as president of Southwestern Seminary. It was Leggett who paid to have the inaugural address published.

55. L. R. Scarborough to Ollie Pender, 6 December 1922. SC, 23.
56. Scarborough, "The Evolution of a Cowboy," 13, SC, 17.
57. *Ibid.*, 15.
58. *Ibid.*, 14; Also see Dana's chapter "The House That Was Never Built," 48-51.
59. Baylor University Report Card, 25 March 1888, SC, 18. The Baylor report card assigns the following scores for Scarborough's first term: Algebra, 98; Latin, 94; Rhetoric, 91; Elocution, 90; Arithmetic, 100; Penmanship, 89; Orthography, 90.
60. Erisophian Literary Society Bulletin, SC, 19.
61. "Lee Rutland Scarborough," SC, 22; Scarborough also received an honorary Doctor of Divinity degree from Baylor on 24 June 1908, SC, 20.
62. Scarborough, "The Evolution of a Cowboy," 16, SC, 17.
63. *Ibid.*
64. Scarborough to Pender, SC, 23.
65. L. R. Scarborough to Horace I. Trout, 26 February 1920. SC, 23.
66. "Lee Rutland Scarborough," SC, 22.
67. Scarborough to Trout. SC, 23.
68. Scarborough to Pender. SC, 23.
69. Dana, 47.
70. Scarborough, "The Evolution of a Cowboy," 20, SC, 17, places his brother in New Mexico. Dana, 15, names Arizona as the site of the event. Since neither Arizona nor New Mexico had achieved statehood in 1900, both writers are probably referring to the same territory.
71. Scarborough, "The Evolution of a Cowboy," 23, SC, 17.
72. *Ibid.*
73. Quoted in Dana, 55.
74. Scarborough, "The Evolution of a Cowboy," 25, SC, 17.
75. "Lee Rutland Scarborough," SC, 22.
76. Scarborough, "The Evolution of a Cowboy," 22, SC, 17.
77. Scarborough, "About My Call to Preach," SC, 1.
78. Scarborough to Trout. SC, 23.
79. L. R. Scarborough to Rev. and Mrs. George Scarborough, 19 April 1896. SC, 27. Scarborough adds: "You will pardon me if I seem overjoyed, or enthusiastic beyond prudence. Just remember, please, that the current of a new life has broken its peaceful waters in upon my soul and all things seem to glitter with the radiance of heavenly happiness. I am no more an ambitious, aspiring, over-studious applicant for honors at the bar of the law, but am an humble, feeble, weak, unprepared, yet joyful aspirant after usefulness in God's kingdom."
80. George W. Scarborough to L. R. Scarborough, 28 April 1896. SC, 11.
81. Scarborough to Trout. SC, 23.
82. Scarborough to Pender. SC, 23; Cf. Dana, 72.
83. Scarborough, "The Evolution of a Cowboy," 39, SC, 17. George Scarborough died during the Cameron pastorate in 1899.
84. *Ibid.*
85. Dana, 63-64; Cf. Baptist Biography File, Archives, A. Webb Roberts Library, Southwestern Baptist Theological Seminary, Fort Worth, Texas, s.v. "Scarborough, Lee Rutland."

86. Scarborough, "The Evolution of a Cowboy," 31-32, SC, 17.
87. "Lee Rutland Scarborough," SC, 22.
88. Dana, 67.
89. Scarborough, "The Evolution of a Cowboy," 33, SC, 17.
90. "Lee Rutland Scarborough," SC, 22. The Scarborough children were George Warren, Euna Lee, Lawrence Rutland, Neppie, Ada Beth, and William Byron.
91. See Dana, 63-71.
92. "Lee Rutland Scarborough," SC, 22.
93. First Baptist Church, Abilene, Minutes, 30 July 1902.
94. Scarborough, "The Evolution of a Cowboy," 39, SC, 17.
95. *Ibid.*
96. Dana, 74.
97. *Ibid.*, 93.
98. B. F. Riley, *History of the Baptists of Texas* (Dallas: By the author, 1907), 327-328.
99. First Baptist Church, Abilene, Minutes, 27 August 1902.
100. *Ibid.*, 24 September 1902.
101. Dana, 93.
102. *Ibid.*
103. Scarborough to Trout. SC, 23.
104. *Ibid.*
105. Dana, 95.
106. Scarborough to Trout. SC, 23.
107. Scarborough, "The Evolution of a Cowboy," 42, SC, 17.
108. Dana, 74.

CHAPTER 2

1. Norman Wade Cox and Judson Boyce Allen, eds., *Encyclopedia of Southern Baptists* (Nashville: Broadman Press, 1958), s.v. "Carroll, Benajah Harvey," by Franklin M. Segler.
2. Robert A. Baker, *The Blossoming Desert: A Concise History of Texas Baptists* (Waco: Word Books, 1970), 181.
3. Robert A. Baker, *Tell the Generations Following: A History of Southwestern Baptist Theological Seminary, 1908-1983* (Nashville: Broadman Press, 1983), 115.
4. *Ibid.*, 117.
5. L. R. Scarborough, *A Modern School of the Prophets* (Nashville: Broadman Press, 1939), 106. This is the first published history of Southwestern Seminary. Of course, the author had firsthand knowledge of every aspect of the institution's history.
6. L. R. Scarborough, "Certain Facts Concerning the History of the Southwestern Baptist Theological Seminary," 4, Archives, A. Webb Roberts Library, Southwestern Baptist Theological Seminary, Fort Worth, Texas. This is an unpublished manuscript written by Scarborough in 1932 possibly in preparation for his 1939 history of the Seminary. He admits at the outset that he is "writing largely from memory."
7. Southwestern Baptist Theological Seminary Board of Trustee Minutes, 8 May 1908.

Notes

8. *Ibid.*; Cf. Scarborough, "Certain Facts Concerning the History of the Southwestern Baptist Theological Seminary," who adds James J. Reeve to the list of charter faculty members.

9. B. H. Carroll to L. R. Scarborough, 1 November 1906, SC, 58.

10. *Ibid.* Records do not indicate the identity of the second person to whom Carroll refers.

11. B. H. Carroll to L. R. Scarborough, 11 January 1908, SC, 59; B. H. Carroll to L. R. Scarborough, 11 January 1908, SC, 60.

12. Carroll to Scarborough, SC, 60.

13. *Ibid.*

14. *Ibid.*

15. Dana, 80.

16. *Ibid.*, 83–84; Cf. L. R. Scarborough to B. H. Carroll, 24 February 1908, SC, 61. Also see the B. H. Carroll Collection, 279, Archives, A. Webb Roberts Library, Southwestern Baptist Theological Seminary, Fort Worth, Texas.

17. Jeff D. Ray, "The First Faculty of the Seminary," 15, Archives, A. Webb Roberts Library, Southwestern Baptist Theological Seminary, Fort Worth, Texas.

18. L. R. Scarborough, "The Southwestern Seminary's Department of Evangelism," 1, SC, 74.

19. Scarborough, *A Modern School of the Prophets*, 133.

20. Scarborough, "Certain Facts Concerning the History of the Southwestern Baptist Theological Seminary," 10.

21. *Ibid.*, 9.

22. Baker, *Tell the Generations Following*, 147, says that Dallas was "the denominational center of Texas Baptists."

23. *Ibid.*

24. Scarborough, "Certain Facts Concerning the History of the Southwestern Baptist Theological Seminary," 9–10.

25. *Ibid.*, 10.

26. Baker, *Tell the Generations Following*, 148.

27. Scarborough, "Certain Facts Concerning the History of the Southwestern Baptist Theological Seminary," 11.

28. Scarborough, *A Modern School of the Prophets*, 64.

29. Scarborough, "Certain Facts Concerning the History of the Southwestern Baptist Theological Seminary," 12.

30. *Ibid.*

31. Southwestern Baptist Theological Seminary Board of Trustee Minutes, 2 November 1909.

32. *Ibid.*, 13 November 1909; Cf. J. M. Carroll, *A History of Texas Baptists* (Dallas: Baptist Standard Publishing Co., 1923), 984, who writes that the "raising, collecting and administering of the building fund donated by the people of Fort Worth and from other sources, were entirely handled by L. R. Scarborough."

33. Scarborough, *A Modern School of the Prophets*, 133.

34. *Ibid.*, 134.

35. Southwestern Baptist Theological Seminary Board of Trustee Minutes, 18 January 1910.

36. L. R. Scarborough to B. H. Carroll, 21 February 1910, B. H. Carroll Collection, 280.

37. *Ibid.*
38. L. R. Scarborough to B. H. Carroll, 3 March 1910, B. H. Carroll Collection, 280; Cf. Scarborough, *A Modern School of the Prophets*, 76, which says that the first Seminary building was named in honor of Fort Worth because of the generosity of its citizens.
39. L. R. Scarborough to B. H. Carroll, 4 March 1910, B. H. Carroll Collection, 280.
40. *Ibid.*
41. Records are scant concerning the number of times the conference met. It may have only been the one meeting of 1911. In his history of the Seminary, Baker (*Tell the Generations Following*) makes no mention of the conference.
42. Scarborough to Carroll, 4 March 1910.
43. Scarborough, "Certain Facts Concerning the History of the Southwestern Baptist Theological Seminary," 23.
44. Baker, *Tell the Generations Following*, 165–166.
45. Scarborough, "Certain Facts Concerning the History of the Southwestern Baptist Theological Seminary," 23.
46. Southwestern Baptist Theological Seminary Board of Trustee Minutes, 29 May 1913.
47. Scarborough, "Certain Facts Concerning the History of the Southwestern Baptist Theological Seminary," 23.
48. *Ibid.*
49. Southwestern Baptist Theological Seminary Board of Trustee Minutes, 20 November 1913.
50. *Ibid.*, 27 May 1914.
51. *Ibid.*, 16 November 1914.
52. *Ibid.*, 9 February 1915.
53. Baker, *Tell the Generations Following*, 198, names 28 May 1915 as the inauguration date. The program bulletin for the installation, however, is dated 8 April 1915.
54. Bulletin, "Installation of Lee Rutland Scarborough, President Elect," 8 April 1915, SC 110.
55. L. R. Scarborough, "The Primal Test of Theological Education," SC, 111.
56. *Ibid.*, 4.
57. *Ibid.*
58. *Ibid.*
59. *Ibid.*, 5.
60. *Ibid.*, 13–15.
61. Scarborough, *A Modern School of the Prophets*, 142. The cooperating states were New Mexico, Louisiana, Oklahoma, Mississippi, Florida, Southern Illinois, Tennessee, Kentucky, Arkansas, and Missouri.
62. *Ibid.*
63. *Ibid.* There is some discrepancy over dating at this point. Scarborough gives 17 May 1918 as the board meeting which empowered him to act. Baker, *Tell the Generations Following*, 237, says that a committee was appointed by the trustees on 23 May 1917.
64. Scarborough, *A Modern School of the Prophets*, 143; Cf. Baker, 237.

Notes

65. Carroll, *A History of Texas Baptists*, 987.
66. Scarborough, *A Modern School of the Prophets*, 144–145 recounts the resolution in its entirety.
67. Southwestern Baptist Theological Seminary Board of Trustee Minutes, 14 May 1924. The committee included O.S Lattimore, J. B. Tidwell, and Scarborough.
68. Baker, *Tell the Generations Following*, 238.
69. L. R. Scarborough, "What the Southwestern Baptist Theological Seminary Can Do for Southern Baptists and What Southern Baptists Can Do for the Seminary," 2, SC, 54.
70. *Ibid.*, 3.
71. Carroll, *A History of Texas Baptists*, 982.
72. L. R. Scarborough, "The Southwestern Baptist Seminary," 2, SC, 137.
73. *Ibid.*, 10.
74. Baker, *Tell the Generations Following*, 201.
75. Scarborough, *A Modern School of the Prophets*, 112.
76. Baker, *Tell the Generations Following*, 201.
77. *Ibid.*, 202.
78. Southwestern Baptist Theological Seminary Board of Trustee Minutes, 14 May 1930.
79. *Ibid.*, 26 March 1931.
80. *Ibid.*, 13 May 1931.
81. *Ibid.*, 13 May 1932; Cf. George W. Truett to L. R. Scarborough, 2 October 1934, George W. Truett Collection, 1209, Archives, A. Webb Roberts Library, Southwestern Baptist Theological Seminary, Fort Worth Texas. Truett writes: "Either as *Churches* or as *individuals*, all of us should now aid the noble Seminary. It is one of the most vitally valuable assets in all the world, for the furtherance of Christ's cause in Texas, in the Southland, in America, and throughout all the world. Every one of us should hail it as a privilege to *make worthy gifts* to so glorious an agency for the extension of Christ's cause."
82. Southwestern Baptist Theological Seminary Board of Trustee Minutes, 15 February 1923.
83. L. R. Scarborough to "Former Student," 30 April 1928, SC, 52.
84. Baker, *Tell the Generations Following*, 171.
85. Southwestern Baptist Theological Seminary Board of Trustee Minutes, 29 September 1911.
86. For a more detailed description of the streetcar project, see W. W. Barnes, "Arrival on the Hill," 8–11, W. W. Barnes Collection, Archives, A. Webb Roberts Library, Southwestern Baptist Theological Seminary, Fort Worth, Texas.
87. Mrs. George E. Cowden to L. R. Scarborough, 12 February 1925, Trustee Minute Book 2.
88. Baker, *Tell the Generations Following*, 249.
89. L. R. Scarborough, "History of the Seminary Valley Citrus Fruit Orchard," 1–2, SC, 122.
90. *Ibid.*, 6.
91. *Ibid.*, 7–8.
92. Southwestern Baptist Theological Seminary Board of Trustee Minutes, 16 May 1934.

93. Scarborough, "Citrus Fruit Orchard," 9.

94. *Encyclopedia of Southern Baptists*, 1958 ed., s.v. "Hundred Thousand Club."

95. Baker, *Tell the Generations Following*, 259. Even by 1938 the Seminary was experiencing an alleviation of the debt burden and hope for a brighter future. Scarborough reported to the board of trustees that it was "the best year of the Seminary for many years, debts reduced $50,000, salaries paid promptly every month, 614 students enrolled from a wide area, more than 90 per cent of them college students, a healthy faculty, an enthusiastic Seminary, a hot-hearted force on Seminary Hill going after the lost and training a competent leadership for the churches," Trustee Minutes, 12 May 1938.

96. L. R. Scarborough, "The Appeal of a Great Program," 1, SC, 39.

97. L. R. Scarborough, "Southwestern Seminary Deserves to be Well Endowed," 2, SC, 100.

98. *Ibid.*

99. Dana, 138.

100. Scarborough, *A Modern School of the Prophets*, 117.

101. *Ibid.*, 128.

102. Southwestern Baptist Theological Seminary Board of Trustee Minutes, 14 May 1942.

103. Tom J. Nettles, *The Oral Memoirs of Robert A. Baker* (Dallas: Baptist General Convention of Texas, 1981), 165.

104. *Ibid.*, 31.

105. L. R. Scarborough, "A Brief Review of the Seminary and My Resignation," 3, Archives, A. Webb Roberts Library, Southwestern Baptist Theological Seminary, Fort Worth, Texas.

106. *Ibid.*, 5–6.

107. Dana, 142.

108. *Encyclopedia of Southern Baptists*, 1958 ed., s.v. "Norris, John Franklyn." The unusual life and career of Norris are not covered here in detail, but only those aspects which relate to his struggle with Scarborough.

109. Baker, *Tell the Generations Following*, 178.

110. *Ibid.*, 178–179.

111. *Ibid.*, 181.

112. The 75 Million Campaign operated from 1919 to 1924 as a fund-raising program of the Southern Baptist Convention. The Campaign, which is at the heart of Scarborough's New Denominationalism, is the focus of Chapter 3.

113. Baker, *The Blossoming Desert*, 198.

114. Baker, *Tell the Generations Following*, 222.

115. L. R. Scarborough, "A Statement and A Resolution," SC, 149.

116. *Ibid.*, 1.

117. *Ibid.*, 5.

118. *Ibid.*, 4.

119. Baker, *Tell the Generations Following*, 222.

120. Scarborough, "A Statement and A Resolution," 8.

121. *Ibid.*

122. Baker, *Tell the Generations Following*, 225.

123. L. R. Scarborough, "Radio Address," c. 1927, 4, SC, 642.

124. *Ibid.*, 5.
125. H. C. McCart to "Whom it May Concern," 1 December 1927, SC, 666.
126. *Ibid.*
127. L. R. Scarborough to J. Frank Norris, 7 December 1921.
128. J. Frank Norris to L. R. Scarborough, 8 October 1927, SC, 263.
129. *Ibid.*
130. Scarborough, "Radio Address," 9, SC, 642.
131. *Ibid.*; Cf. L. R. Scarborough, "Where the 'Searchlight' Missed It Again," 2, SC, 153.
132. Scarborough, "Radio Address," 10.
133. L. R. Scarborough, "How Is This for a Baptist Church?," 5, SC, 657.
134. In existence from 1919 through 1928, the Education Board promoted Southern Baptist academic institutions. See *Encyclopedia of Southern Baptists*, 1958 ed., s.v. "Education Board."
135. Norris to Scarborough, 8 October 1927.
136. *Ibid.*
137. Scarborough, "Radio Address," 13.
138. James E. Carter, *Cowboys, Cowtown & Crosses: A Centennial History of the Tarrant Baptist Association* (Fort Worth: Tarrant Baptist Association, 1986), 55; Cf. Nettles, 36.
139. J. Frank Norris to L. R. Scarborough, 12 January 1924, SC, 261.
140. L. R. Scarborough to J. Frank Norris, 21 January 1924, SC, 261.
141. *Ibid.*
142. Carter, 55.
143. L. R. Scarborough and others, "A Challenge," 1, SC, 643; Cf. J. Frank Norris to L. R. Scarborough, 28 October 1924, SC, 261. Norris writes: "I notice where you indicate or threaten that my seat is going to be challenged at the coming convention in Dallas. In order that you may be thoroughly informed I here now announce that I am going as a messenger of the First Baptist Church, and I challenge you to make your challenge!"
144. Baker, *Tell the Generations Following*, 228.
145. Scarborough to Norris, 21 January 1924.
146. Scarborough, "How Is This for a Baptist Church?," 1.
147. *Ibid.*, 2.
148. L. R. Scarborough, "Illustration of the Doctrine of Depravity," 1, SC, 644.
149. L. R. Scarborough, "The Fruits of Norrisism," SC, 652. The tract is undated, but was probably written at the end of 1927 or the beginning of 1928.
150. *Ibid.*
151. *Ibid.*
152. *Ibid.*
153. *Ibid.*
154. Norris to Scarborough, 28 October 1924.
155. W. W. Barnes, "Denominational Leader," *Southwestern News* III (May 1945): 2.

CHAPTER 3

1. The Interchurch World Movement, which began at the close of World War I, attempted to form a union of Protestants around the world for the purpose of missions and social work. It was a failed effort, however, and was dismantled by 1920. See Mark A. Noll, ed., *Eerdmans Handbook to Christianity in America* (Grand Rapids: William B. Eerdmans Publishing Co., 1983), 373–374.

2. W. W. Barnes, *The Southern Baptist Convention, 1845–1953* (Nashville: Broadman Press, 1954), 221.

3. *Encyclopedia of Southern Baptists*, 1958 ed., s.v. "Executive Committee of the Southern Baptist Convention."

4. *Ibid.*

5. Barnes, 221–222.

6. L. R. Scarborough, "From Our Knees Out to the Nations," *Baptist Standard*, 19 June 1919, 1.

7. L. R. Scarborough, "The Steady March of a Great People," *Baptist Standard*, 5 June 1919, 6. Scarborough exclaimed: "My deliberate judgment is that no religious people ever had a greater convention than Southern Baptists had at Atlanta. . . . The spirit of the convention was glorious."

8. Southern Baptist Convention *Annual* (1919), 17.

9. *Ibid.*, 23.

10. H. Leon McBeth, *A Sourcebook for Baptist Heritage* (Nashville: Broadman Press, 1990), 448.

11. Southern Baptist Convention *Annual* (1919), 82.

12. Scarborough, "From Our Knees Out to the Nations," 1.

13. L. R. Scarborough, *Marvels of Divine Leadership, or the Story of the Southern Baptist 75 Million Campaign* (Nashville: Sunday School Board of the Southern Baptist Convention, 1920), 18, lists eighteen members of the Commission: "Dr. Geo. W. Truett, Texas; Dr. H. L. Winburn, Arkansas; Dr. J. E. Dillard, Alabama; Dr. John E. Briggs, District of Columbia; Dr. W. A. Hobson, Florida; Dr. F. C. McConnell, Georgia; Rev. E. W. Reeder, Illinois; Mr. Geo. E. Hays, Kentucky; Dr. M. E. Dodd, Louisiana; Hon. Joshua Levering, Maryland; Rev. W. A. Hewitt, Mississippi; Hon. E. W. Stephens, Missouri; Rev. J. W. Bruner, New Mexico; Judge Gilbert T. Stephenson, North Carolina; Rev. E. L. Compere, Oklahoma; Mr. J. H. Anderson, Tennessee; Mr. C. B. Bobo, South Carolina, and Dr. Geo. W. McDaniel, Virginia."

14. *Ibid.*, 24–25.

15. *Ibid.*, 26.

16. Quoted in Dana, 108.

17. Scarborough, "From Our Knees Out to the Nations," 1.

18. *Ibid.*

19. *Ibid.*

20. Scarborough, *Marvels of Divine Leadership*, 28.

21. George W. Truett, "Thinking in Millions," *Baptist Standard*, 12 June 1919, 1.

22. Scarborough, *Marvels of Divine Leadership*, 36.

23. L. R. Scarborough, "Two of the Greatest Baptist Days," *Baptist Standard*, 10 July 1919, 5.

24. *Ibid.*

25. Barnes, 224.
26. Scarborough, *Marvels of Divine Leadership*, 26.
27. Dana, 103.
28. Southern Baptist Convention, *Annual* (1919), 82.
29. Baptist 75 Million Campaign, "Baptist Campaigner," September 1919, SC, 546.
30. *Ibid.* Others on the staff were Mrs. Janie Cree Bose, WMU Organizer; Victor Masters, stereopticon; Sarah Paris, secretary; Burney Bennett, secretary; Frank Burkhalter, secular press liaison; Burton Stoddard, J. A. Kirtley, and W. H. Carr in the service field.
31. Scarborough, *Marvels of Divine Leadership*, 39.
32. George W. Truett, "Mighty Meaning of Thirty Days," *Baptist Standard*, 30 October 1919, 1.
33. "Baptist Campaigner," SC, 546.
34. *Ibid.*
35. Scarborough, *Marvels of Divine Leadership*, 40.
36. "Baptist Campaigner," SC, 546.
37. L. R. Scarborough, "The Deeper Significance of the Campaign," *Western Recorder*, 6 November 1919, 1.
38. *Ibid.*
39. Dana, 103.
40. *75 Million Campaign State Papers*, Archives, A. Webb Roberts Library, Southwestern Baptist Theological Seminary, Fort Worth, Texas.
41. Scarborough, *Marvels of Divine Leadership*, 41; Cf. "Baptist Campaigner," SC, 546.
42. Scarborough, *Marvels of Divine Leadership*, 41.
43. J. B. Gambrell, "Several Important Matters," *Baptist Standard*, 18 September 1919, 5.
44. I. E. Reynolds, "When Millions Come Pouring In," *SBC 75 Million Campaign File*, Archives, A. Webb Roberts Library, Southwestern Baptist Theological Seminary, Fort Worth, Texas. The hymn contains five verses and a chorus.
45. Scarborough, *Marvels of Divine Leadership*, 41.
46. T. B. Ray, "Evangelism – Enlightenment – Enlistment," SC, 536.
47. *Ibid.*, 5.
48. L. R. Scarborough, "Our Greatest and All-Inclusive Need," in Ray, 31.
49. D. F. Green, "Soda Water, Cigars and Campaign Pledges," *SBC 75 Million Campaign File*.
50. *Ibid.*
51. "A Vital Discussion Between Two Business Men," *SBC 75 Million Campaign File*.
52. *Ibid.*
53. L. R. Scarborough, "Baptists Facing a Big Task," 1, SC, 526.
54. *Ibid.*, 2.
55. L. R. Scarborough, "Eternal Matters Involved in the 75 Million Campaign," 1, SC, 535.
56. *Ibid.*, 2.
57. Scarborough, "The Deeper Significance of the Campaign," 1.
58. Scarborough, "Baptists Facing a Big Task," 2, SC, 526.

59. Scarborough, *Marvels of Divine Leadership*, 43.
60. *Ibid.*, 43-46. The stewardship emphasis was one of the lasting effects of the Campaign. It remains a practice in many Southern Baptist churches for one month in the fall to be set aside for stewardship sermons. See Barnes, 224.
61. Dana, 100.
62. "Baptist Campaigner," SC, 546; Cf. L. R. Scarborough, "The Steady March of a Great People," *Baptist Standard*, 5 June 1919, 6.
63. Scarborough, *Marvels of Divine Leadership*, 49.
64. I.. R. Scarborough, *Recruits for World Conquests* (New York: Fleming H. Revell Co., 1914); Cf. Dana, 86-87.
65. L. R. Scarborough, "Report of Campaign Commission," SC, 551.
66. "Baptist Campaigner," SC, 546.
67. Scarborough, *Marvels of Divine Leadership*, 60-62.
68. I. E. Gates, "The 75 Million Drive Not for Money Alone," *Baptist Standard*, 25 September 1919, 5.
69. F. S. Groner, "On the Eve of Battle," *Baptist Standard*, 27 November 1919, 1.
70. L. R. Scarborough, "Campaign Encouragements," *Western Recorder*, 11 September 1919, 2.
71. L. R. Scarborough, "Pressing the Battle to Victory Gates," *Baptist Standard*, 27 November 1919, 2.
72. Dana, 103.
73. Scarborough, "Our Greatest and All-Inclusive Need," 31.
74. L. R. Scarborough, "The Baptist Pot is Boiling," *Western Recorder*, 4 September 1919, 3.
75. Scarborough, "Campaign Encouragements," 2.
76. Scarborough, "The Baptist Pot is Boiling," 3.
77. Scarborough, "Report of Campaign Commission," 4.
78. Scarborough, *Marvels of Divine Leadership*, 96.
79. *Ibid.*
80. *Ibid.*, 105.
81. *Ibid.*, 111.
82. Dana, 103.
83. Scarborough, *Marvels of Divine Leadership*, 96.
84. Scarborough, "Report of Campaign Commission," 7.
85. Scarborough, "A Further Word About the Campaign," 1, SC, 538.
86. Scarborough, "Report of Campaign Commission," 5.
87. Southern Baptist Convention, *Annual* (1920), 51.
88. Millard A. Jenkins, "Assets of the Great Baptist Campaign," *Baptist Standard*, 13 May 1920, 6.
89. L. R. Scarborough, "A Further Word About the Campaign," *Biblical Recorder*, 7 January 1920, 5.
90. Southern Baptist Convention, *Annual* (1920), 48-59.
91. *Ibid.*, 48.
92. *Ibid.*, 48-50.
93. *Ibid.*, 51; Cf. Scarborough, "Report of Campaign Commission," 6-7.
94. Southern Baptist Convention, *Annual* (1920), 54.
95. *Ibid.*

96. E. C. Routh, "The Southern Baptist Convention," *Baptist Standard*, 20 May 1920, 5. The greater participation in the SBC between 1919 and 1920 was evidenced by the increase in attendance at the annual meeting. At the 1919 Convention in Atlanta, 4,224 messengers registered. The number of messengers in 1920 almost doubled as 8,359 gathered in Washington, D.C. See Barnes, Appendix B.

97. Southern Baptist Convention, *Annual* (1920), 58.

98. *Ibid.*

99. As early as January 1920, Scarborough was already considering a Conservation Commission. He wrote: "Now that God and a co-operating brotherhood have given us the money for a new era and an enlarged work, we must go forward with a mighty, aggressive, constructive program for the right *conservation of what we have already won* [author emphasis]." See L. R. Scarborough, "Our General Director's Victory Message," *Home and Foreign Fields*, January 1920, 1, *SBC 75 Million Campaign File*.

100. L. R. Scarborough to "Brother," November 1922, SC, 533; Cf. Southern Baptist Convention, *Annual* (1925), 22–25.

101. L. R. Scarborough, "Address delivered on 75 Million Campaign," 1 December 1921, SC, 525.

102. Barnes, 231.

103. "Financial Statement for First Two Years of Campaign," SC, 537.

104. Scarborough, "Address delivered on 75 Million Campaign," 15.

105. L. R. Scarborough, "What You Have Missed," *SBC 75 Million Campaign File*.

106. *Ibid.*; Also see "Why Every Baptist Should Have a Part in the 75 Million Campaign," *Campaign Talking Points*, 1 November 1922, SC, 531.

107. L. R. Scarborough, "God's Storehouse and His Challenge to Baptists," *SBC 75 Million Campaign File*.

108. *Ibid.*

109. L. R. Scarborough to "Brother," November 1922, SC, 533.

110. "Southern Baptist Clip Sheet," 21 July 1924, *SBC 75 Million Campaign File*.

111. Conservation Commission, "Baptist Dollars on Duty," *SBC 75 Million Campaign File*.

112. *Ibid.*

113. Dana, 107.

114. L. R. Scarborough, "Baptists Facing the Future," 1, SC, 527.

115. *Ibid.*, 2.

116. Southern Baptist Convention, *Annual* (1925), 22–25.

117. *Ibid.*, 23.

118. *Ibid.*, 25.

119. Scarborough, "Baptists Facing the Future," 5, SC, 527.

120. L. R. Scarborough, "My Gratitude to God and the Brotherhood of Baptists," 1, SC, 539.

121. L. M. Aldridge, "Baptist 75-Million Campaign Success Has Stirred Entire Religious World," *World-Wide News*, 18 October 1922, SC, 559.

122. Conservation Commission, "Baptist Dollars on Duty," *SBC 75 Million Campaign File*.

123. Scarborough, "Baptists Facing the Future," 5, SC, 527.
124. Scarborough, *Marvels of Divine Leadership*, 116-125.
125. *Ibid.*, 116-117.
126. *Ibid.*, 117.
127. *Ibid.*, 122.
128. L. R. Scarborough, "Is Cooperation a New Testament Doctrine?," 3, SC, 401.
129. L. R. Scarborough, "The Heresy of Non-Co-operation," SC, 402.
130. *Ibid.*, 1.
131. L. R. Scarborough, "The Peril of Lop-Sided Cooperation," SC, 403.
132. *Ibid.*, 1.
133. L. R. Scarborough, "Article 19 on Co-operation," SC, 398.
134. For a text of the 1925 confession, see Robert A. Baker, *A Baptist Source Book, with Particular Reference to Southern Baptists* (Nashville: Broadman Press, 1966), 200-205.
135. Jeff Ray, "Introduction," in *A Modern School of the Prophets*, 12.
136. Robert A. Baker, "The Cooperative Program in Historical Perspective," *Baptist History and Heritage* 10 (July 1975): 173, states "By far the most influential factor in the development of the Cooperative Program of 1925 was the 75 Million Campaign of 1919-24."
137. Southern Baptist Convention, *Annual* (1925), 26.
138. *Ibid.*, 25.
139. "Report and Recommendations of Headquarters Committee to Full Program Commission," 11 May 1925, 6, *SBC 75 Million Campaign File*.
140. *Ibid.*, 5.
141. Baker, "The Cooperative Program in Historical Perspective," 176.
142. Timothy George, "The Southern Baptist Cooperative Program: Heritage and Challenge," *Baptist History and Heritage* 20 (April 1985): 8.
143. Southern Baptist Convention, *Annual* (1925), 25.
144. Scarborough, *Marvels of Divine Leadership*, 116.

CHAPTER 4

1. L. R. Scarborough, *Recruits for World Conquests* (New York: Fleming H. Revell Co., 1914); idem, *With Christ After the Lost* (Nashville: Sunday School Board of the Southern Baptist Convention, 1919); idem, *Endued to Win* (Nashville: Sunday School Board of the Southern Baptist Convention, 1922).
2. Barnes, 233-234.
3. *Encyclopedia of Southern Baptists*, 1958 ed., s.v. "Evangelism, Home Mission Board Program of."
4. *Ibid.*
5. *Ibid.*
6. L. R. Scarborough, "Southern Baptists and Evangelism," SC, 22.
7. *Ibid.*
8. *Ibid.*
9. *Ibid.*
10. *Ibid.*
11. "Baptist Campaigner," SC, 546.
12. Southern Baptist Convention, *Annual* (1921), 28.

Notes

13. Barnes, 233.
14. Southern Baptist Convention, *Annual* (1921), 402.
15. *Ibid.*
16. *Ibid.*, 33; Cf. Barnes, 233.
17. Scarborough, *Recruits for World Conquests*, 23-31.
18. *Ibid.*, 24.
19. *Ibid.*, 26-27.
20. L. R. Scarborough, *How Jesus Won Men* (Nashville: Sunday School Board of the Southern Baptist Convention, 1926), 48.
21. *Ibid.*, 48-49.
22. L. R. Scarborough, "Evangelizing Our Schools," SC, 421.
23. L. R. Scarborough, "Evangelism in Baptist Schools," 5, SC, 418; Cf. idem, "Soul Winning in Education," SC, 435.
24. L. R. Scarborough, "Our Seminaries and Evangelism," SC, 545.
25. L. R. Scarborough, "A Statement and Recommendation on a Southwide Campaign for Soul Winning," 6, SC, 439.
26. L. R. Scarborough, "Training an Evangelistic Ministry," 8, SC, 443.
27. *Ibid.*
28. Scarborough, "A Statement and Recommendation on a Southwide Campaign for Soul Winning," 6.
29. Scarborough, "Training an Evangelistic Ministry," 9.
30. Scarborough, "Our Seminaries and Evangelism," 6.
31. Scarborough, *Recruits for World Conquests*, 58.
32. *Ibid.*, 64-65.
33. Scarborough, "Training an Evangelistic Ministry," 7.
34. Scarborough, "Our Seminaries and Evangelism," 4.
35. L. R. Scarborough, "Department of Evangelism," 1, SC, 65.
36. *Ibid.*
37. L. R. Scarborough, "The Southwestern Seminary's Department of Evangelism," 1, SC, 74.
38. Southwestern Baptist Theological Seminary Board of Trustee Minutes, 27 May 1915.
39. L. R. Scarborough, "Evangelism – Winter Term, 1913-1914," SC, 626.
40. *Ibid.*, 1.
41. L. R. Scarborough, "The Terms of Power: A Study in the Holy Spirit's Evangelism," 7, SC, 608.
42. L. R. Scarborough, "Lecture No. 11, PENTECOST," 1, SC, 631. This may be the only written document where Scarborough espouses a landmark view of Baptist history. In one brief statement, he shares his belief that "there was a Baptist Church in Jerusalem at this time."
43. *Ibid.*
44. Scarborough, "Evangelism – Winter Term, 1913-1914," 1.
45. Scarborough, "The Terms of Power: A Study in the Holy Spirit's Evangelism," 7.
46. L. R. Scarborough, "Paul the World's Greatest Evangelist," SC, 630.
47. L. R. Scarborough, "Class Notes," SC, 622.
48. *Ibid.*; Cf. Scarborough, "Paul the World's Greatest Evangelist," 4.
49. L. R. Scarborough, "Paul the Winning Preacher," SC, 629.

50. Scarborough, "Paul the World's Greatest Evangelist," 1.
51. Scarborough, "Paul the Winning Preacher," 1.
52. Scarborough, "Paul the World's Greatest Evangelist," 1.
53. Scarborough, "Paul the Winning Preacher," 1.
54. Scarborough, "Class Notes," SC, 622.
55. L. R. Scarborough, "Evangelism the Heart of the New Testament," SC, 422.
56. *Ibid.*, 1.
57. L. R. Scarborough, "Regeneration's Primary Obligation – Soul Winning," 14, SC, 607.
58. L. R. Scarborough, "Principles in the Commission Applied to Evangelism," SC, 633. This lecture was first delivered to an evangelism class at Southwestern Seminary on 23 February 1916.
59. *Ibid.*
60. *Ibid.*
61. *Ibid.*; Cf. Scarborough, *Recruits for World Conquests*, 92.
62. Scarborough, "Regeneration's Primary Obligation – Soul Winning," 13.
63. Scarborough, "Class Notes," SC, 622.
64. Scarborough, "Evangelism the Heart of the New Testament," 2-3.
65. L. R. Scarborough, "Methods for Harvesting the Results of a Revival Meeting," 1, SC, 427.
66. Scarborough, "Class Notes," SC, 622. Scarborough taught that revival preaching should be "positive, personal, and persuasive."
67. Scarborough, "Methods for Harvesting the Results of a Revival Meeting," 1.
68. L. R. Scarborough, "Constructive Evangelism," 2, SC, 416.
69. *Ibid.*
70. L. R. Scarborough, "Some Soul-Winning Suggestions," SC, 433.
71. L. R. Scarborough, "God's Call and Challenge to Southern Baptists," 8, SC, 499.
72. *Ibid.*, 9.
73. L. R. Scarborough, "The Mastery of the Main Thing," 3-4, SC, 425.
74. Scarborough, "Methods for Harvesting the Results of a Revival Meeting," 2.
75. *Ibid.*
76. Scarborough, "Class Notes," SC, 622.
77. Scarborough, "The Mastery of the Main Thing," 2.
78. Scarborough, "God's Call and Challenge to Southern Baptists," 10.
79. Dana, 86.
80. *Ibid.*, 87, reports that by 1942 more than 6,000 Southwestern students had been influenced by this book. It was also used in other American theological institutions, as well as being required reading in a number of foreign seminaries. By the early 1950s, the text retained such popularity that it was updated and redistributed. See L. R. Scarborough, *With Christ After the Lost*, revised by E. D. Head (Nashville: Broadman Press, 1952).
81. Scarborough, *With Christ After the Lost*, 63.
82. *Ibid.*, 67.

Notes

83. *Ibid.*, 18.
84. *Ibid.*, 41. One should note some change in language between the 1919 and 1952 editions. For example, E. D. Head, 32, inserted "burning passion" for the original "consuming spiritual passion."
85. Scarborough, *With Christ After the Lost*, 169-170.
86. *Ibid.*, 175.
87. *Ibid.*
88. *Ibid.*, 332.
89. Scarborough, *Endued to Win*, 87.
90. *Ibid.*, 229-230.
91. *Ibid.*, 155.
92. C. E. Matthews, "The Evangelist," *Southwestern News* III (May 1945): 7, shares his personal knowledge of Scarborough's devotion to evangelism. "It is my belief," writes Matthews, "that he was probably the greatest evangelist Southern Baptists ever produced. . . . Dr. Scarborough practiced soul winning almost constantly. . . . [He] probably taught the art of soul winning and inspired more people to win others to Christ than any man who ever lived."
93. Scarborough, *How Jesus Won Men*, 48.
94. *Ibid.*
95. L. R. Scarborough, *A Search for Souls* (Nashville: Sunday School Board of the Southern Baptist Convention, 1925), 13.
96. *Ibid.*, 15-16.
97. L. R. Scarborough, *The Tears of Jesus* (New York: George H. Doran Co., 1922), 31.
98. *Ibid.*, 32; Cf. Scarborough, *A Search for Souls*, 61.
99. Scarborough, *Recruits for World Conquests*, 24, reminds the reader of the "human side to a divine call."
100. L. R. Scarborough, *Prepare to Meet God* (Nashville: Sunday School Board of the Southern Baptist Convention, 1922), 93.
101. Scarborough, *A Search for Souls*, 62.
102. L. R. Scarborough, *My Conception of the Gospel Ministry* (Nashville: Sunday School Board of the Southern Baptist Convention, 1935), 58.
103. *Ibid.*, 59.
104. See chapter eleven of *With Christ After the Lost*, "The Evangelistic Church – How to Build One," 146-151.
105. L. R. Scarborough, *Christ's Militant Kingdom* (Nashville: Sunday School Board of the Southern Baptist Convention, 1924), 124.
106. Scarborough, *With Christ After the Lost*, 149-150.
107. L. R. Scarborough, *Ten Spiritual Ships* (Nashville: Sunday School Board of the Southern Baptist Convention, 1927), 75.
108. Scarborough, *Christ's Militant Kingdom*, 124.
109. Dana, 133.

CHAPTER 5

1. Scarborough Chronology, SC, 22.
2. W. W. Barnes, "Denominational Leader," *Southwestern News* III (May 1945): 2.
3. Dana, 74.

Bibliography

Primary Sources

Books

Baker, Robert A. *A Baptist Source Book*. Nashville: Broadman Press, 1966.
Coleman, C. C., et al. *Sermons on the Campaign*. Nashville: Sunday School Board of the Southern Baptist Convention, 1920.
McBeth, H. Leon. *A Source Book for Baptist Heritage*. Nashville: Broadman Press, 1990.
Scarborough, L. R. *Ten Spiritual Ships*. Nashville: Sunday School Board of the Southern Baptist Convention, 1927.
———. *Holy Places and Precious Promises*. New York: George H. Doran Co., 1924.
———. *A Modern School of the Prophets*. Nashville: Broadman Press, 1939.
———. "The World-Will of Jesus Christ." In *Sermons on the Campaign*, ed. I. J. Van Ness. Nashville: Sunday School Board of the Southern Baptist Convention, (192?).
———. *Recruits for World Conquests*. New York: Fleming H. Revell Co., 1914.
———. *The Tears of Jesus*. New York: George H. Doran Co., 1922.
———. *With Christ After the Lost*. Nashville: Sunday School Board of the Southern Baptist Convention, 1919.
———. *Marvels of Divine Leadership, or The Story of the Southern Baptist 75 Million Campaign*. Nashville: Sunday School Board of the Southern Baptist Convention, 1920.
———. *Endued to Win*. Nashville: Sunday School Board of the Southern Baptist Convention, 1922.
———. *After the Resurrection – What?* Grand Rapids: Zondervan Publishing House, 1942.
———. *How Jesus Won Men*. Nashville: Sunday School Board of the Southern Baptist Convention, 1926.
———. *A Blaze of Evangelism Across the Equator*. Nashville: Broadman Press, 1937.
———. *My Conception of the Gospel Ministry*. Nashville: Sunday School Board of the Southern Baptist Convention, 1935.
———. *Prepare to Meet God*. New York: George H. Doran Co., 1922.
———. *Products of Pentecost*. New York: Fleming H. Revell Co., 1934.
———. *Christ's Militant Kingdom*. Nashville: Sunday School Board of the Southern Baptist Convention, 1924.
———. *A Search for Souls*. Nashville: Sunday School Board of the Southern Baptist Convention, 1925.

Collections

Barnes, W. W. *W. W. Barnes Collection.* Archives, A. Webb Roberts Library, Southwestern Baptist Theological Seminary, Fort Worth, Texas.
Carroll, B. H. *B. H. Carroll Collection.* Archives, A. Webb Roberts Library, Southwestern Baptist Theological Seminary, Fort Worth, Texas.
Carroll, J. M. *J. M. Carroll Collection.* Archives, A. Webb Roberts Library, Southwestern Baptist Theological Seminary, Fort Worth, Texas.
Norris, J. Frank. *J. Frank Norris Collection.* Archives, A. Webb Roberts Library, Southwestern Baptist Theological Seminary, Fort Worth, Texas.
Scarborough, L. R. *L. R. Scarborough Collection.* Archives, A. Webb Roberts Library, Southwestern Baptist Theological Seminary, Fort Worth, Texas.
Truett, George W. *George W. Truett Collection.* Archives, A. Webb Roberts Library, Southwestern Baptist Theological Seminary, Fort Worth, Texas.

Articles

Baptist Standard. 1908–1945.
Bryan, O. E. "Concerning Designation." *Western Recorder,* 16 October 1919, 1.
Carver, W. O. "The Campaign and Evangelism." *Western Recorder,* 30 October 1919, 1.
Chambliss, T. W. "Millions for the Master." *Biblical Recorder,* 24 September 1919, 3.
Cullom, W. R. "What Will Be Done with Seventy-Five Millions?" *Biblical Recorder,* 1 October 1919, 4.
Dawson, J. M. "What Shall Become of the 75 Million Fund?" *Baptist Standard,* 16 October 1919, 14.
Derieux, W. T. "Baptist 75 Million Campaign." *Baptist Courier,* 31 July 1919, 1.
Dillard, J. E. "What the 75 Million Campaign Has Demonstrated." *Biblical Recorder,* 24 December 1919, 5.
Edmonds, Richard H. "Baptists are Rich Enough to Do It." *Baptist Courier,* 14 August 1919, 2.
Fort, Allen. "The Baptist Tide Rising." *Biblical Recorder,* 27 August 1919, 1.
Gambrell, J. B. "Our Task — Let Us Perform the Doing of It." *Baptist Standard,* 24 July 1919, 8.
———. "Several Important Matters." *Baptist Standard,* 18 September 1919, 5.
———. "Some Fine Demonstrations." *Baptist Standard,* 25 December 1919, 5.
———. "We Can Win This Way." *Baptist Standard,* 20 November 1919, 5.
Gates, I. E. "The 75 Million Drive Not for Money Alone." *Baptist Standard,* 25 September 1919, 5.
Greer, O. W. "The Uplifting Power of the Campaign." *Western Recorder,* 4 September 1919, 3.
———. "The Unifying Power of the Campaign." *Baptist Courier,* 25 September 1919, 2.
Groner, F. S. "Campaigning with Dr. Truett." *Baptist Standard,* 6 November 1919, 16.
———. "On the Eve of Battle." *Baptist Standard,* 27 November 1919, 1.
Haynes, A. F. "Some Allies on Our Side Helping Us to Succeed in the 75 Million Campaign." *Word and Way,* 13 November 1919, 6–7.
Henderson, J. T. "A Threefold Challenge." *Word and Way,* 28 August 1919, 5.

Bibliography

Hening, B. C. "Soon to Measure the Harvest." *Word and Way*, 27 November 1919, 7.
——. "Volunteer Workers in Baptist 75 Million Campaign." *Word and Way*, 28 August 1919, 4.
——. "Not What Others Are Doing But What We Must Do." *Baptist Courier*, 25 September 1919, 3.
"How the 75 Million Campaign Goes." *Western Recorder*, 18 September 1919, 4–5.
Jenkins, Millard A. "Assets of the Great Baptist Campaign." *Baptist Standard*, 13 May 1920, 6.
Love, J. F. "Men and Money for Foreign Missions." *Word and Way*, 31 July 1919, 4.
McGlothlin, W. J. "Some Final Suggestions for Campaign Workers." *Baptist Courier*, 27 November 1919, 1.
Mullins, E. Y. "Reasons Why Baptists Should Raise $75,000,000." *Baptist Standard*, 11 September 1919, 14.
Norris, J. Frank. "The Greatest Convention in Twenty Years." *The Journal of Texas Baptist History* 1 (1981): 69–77.
Ray, T. B. "Victory Week Message from the Foreign Mission Board." *Biblical Recorder*, 26 November 1919, 3.
Robinson, James. "Publicity and Millions for the Master." *Word and Way*, 24 July 1919, 8.
Routh, E. C. "The Southern Baptist Convention." *Baptist Standard*, 20 May 1920, 5.
Scarborough, L. R. "A Further Word About the Campaign." *Biblical Recorder*, 7 January 1920, 5.
——. "A Prophet's Vision Marvelously Realized." *Word and Way*, 11 September 1919, 4.
——. "Big Things for God." *Biblical Recorder*, 2 July 1919, 1.
——. "Campaign Matters." *Baptist Standard*, 5 February 1920, 7.
——. "Campaign Encouragements." *Western Recorder*, 11 September 1919, 2.
——. "Can We Win? What Our Leaders Say." *Baptist Courier*, 17 July 1919, 2.
——. "Cheering Word from Heroes at the Front." *Biblical Recorder*, 29 October 1919, 1.
——. "Enlisting the Whole Church." *Biblical Recorder*, 8 October 1919, 5.
——. "From Our Knees Out to the Nations." *Baptist Standard*, 19 June 1919, 1.
——. "Looking to Victory – The Thing Most Needful Now." *Baptist Courier*, 21 August 1919, 1.
——. "Matters of Superlative Importance." *Word and Way*, 16 October 1919, 5.
——. "My Soul's Word to Southern Baptists." *Baptist Standard*, 11 September 1919, 1.
——. "Paths to Victory for Millions for the Master." *Baptist Standard*, 3 July 1919, 3.
——. "Paths to Victory for Millions for the Master." *Word and Way*, 3 July 1919, 4.
——. "Pressing the Battle to Victory Gates." *Baptist Standard*, 27 November 1919, 2.
——. "The Baptist Pot is Boiling." *Western Recorder*, 4 September 1919, 3–4.

———. "The Deeper Significance of the Campaign." *Western Recorder*, 6 November 1919, 1.
———. "The Steady March of a Great People." *Baptist Standard*, 5 June 1919, 6.
———. "Trips to Five State Centers and What I Saw." *Word and Way*, 7 August 1919, 4.
———. "Two Other Great Days." *Baptist Standard*, 24 July 1919, 5.
———. "Two of the Greatest Baptist Days." *Baptist Standard*, 10 July 1919, 5.
———. "Victory Tidings." *Baptist Standard*, 20 November 1919, 7.
———. "Watering the Ridges." *Word and Way*, 18 September 1919, 6–7.
———. "What Will the 75 Million Dollar Victory Do for Southern Baptists and the World." *Baptist Standard*, 17 July 1919, 9.
Taylor, J. J. "The 75 Million Dollar Drive." *Biblical Recorder*, 20 August 1919, 5.
Truett, George W. "Announcements Concerning the $75,000,000 Campaign." *Baptist Courier*, 26 June 1919, 2.
———. "Final Words from the Commission." *Word and Way*, 27 November 1919, 9.
———. "Getting a Good Ready." *Baptist Standard*, 31 July 1919, 1.
———. "Mighty Meaning of Thirty Days." *Baptist Standard*, 30 October 1919, 1.
———. "Of the First Importance." *Baptist Standard*, 29 April 1920, 1.
———. "The Closing Hours." *Baptist Standard*, 27 November 1919, 5.
———. "The Campaign Outside of Texas. *Baptist Standard*, 30 October 1919, 5.
———. "Thinking in Millions." *Baptist Standard*, 12 June 1919, 1.
———. "Some Frank Words with Texas Baptists." *The Journal of Texas Baptist History* 1 (1981): 65–68.
Watters, H. E. "Are the Campaign Pledges Scriptural?" *Biblical Recorder*, 12 November 1919, 1.

Annuals

Baptist General Convention of Texas. *Annual*. 1908–1945.
Southern Baptist Convention. *Annual*. 1908–1945.

Pamphlets

Scarborough, L. R. "The Fruits of Norrisism." *The Journal of Texas Baptist History* 1 (1981): 89–97.
———. *The Primal Test of Theological Education: Installation Address of President L. R. Scarborough, D. D., May, 1915*. Fort Worth: Bulletin of the Southwestern Baptist Theological Seminary, 1915.

Unpublished

Minutes. *First Baptist Church, Abilene, Texas, Minutes*. 1901–1908.
Minutes. *Southwestern Baptist Theological Seminary Trustee Minutes*. 1908–1942.
Norris, J. Frank. *J. Frank Norris Papers, 1927–1952*. A. Webb Roberts Library, Southwestern Baptist Theological Seminary, Fort Worth, Texas. Microform.
75 Million Campaign State Papers. Archives, A. Webb Roberts Library, Southwestern Baptist Theological Seminary, Fort Worth, Texas.
SBC 75 Million Campaign Papers. Archives, A. Webb Roberts Library, Southwestern Baptist Theological Seminary, Fort Worth, Texas.

Bibliography

Scarborough, L. R. "Addresses by Dr. L. R. Scarborough." Archives, A. Webb Roberts Library, Southwestern Baptist Theological Seminary, Fort Worth, Texas.
———. "A Brief Review of the Seminary and My Resignation." Archives, A. Webb Roberts Library, Southwestern Baptist Theological Seminary, Fort Worth, Texas.
———. "A Letter to Dr. J. B. Cranfill, June 14, 1927." Archives, A. Webb Roberts Library, Southwestern Baptist Theological Seminary, Fort Worth, Texas.
———. *Department of Evangelism at Southwestern Baptist Theological Seminary.* Fort Worth: Southwestern Baptist Theological Seminary, 1942. Cassette TC 4286.
———. "Certain Facts Concerning the History of the Southwestern Baptist Theological Seminary." Archives, A. Webb Roberts Library, Southwestern Baptist Theological Seminary, Fort Worth, Texas.

Secondary Works

Books

Baker, Robert A. *The Blossoming Desert: A Concise History of Texas Baptists.* Waco: Word Books, 1970.
———. *The Southern Baptist Convention and Its People, 1607-1972.* Nashville: Broadman Press, 1974.
———. *Tell the Generations Following: A History of Southwestern Baptist Theological Seminary, 1908-1983.* Nashville: Broadman Press, 1983.
Barnes, W. W. *The Southern Baptist Convention, 1845-1953.* Nashville: Broadman Press, 1954.
Carroll, J. M. *A History of Texas Baptists.* Dallas: Baptist Standard Publishing Co., 1923.
Carter, James E. *Cowboys, Cowtown & Crosses: A Centennial History of the Tarrant Baptist Association.* Fort Worth: Tarrant Baptist Association, 1986.
Dana, H. E. *Lee Rutland Scarborough: A Life of Service.* Nashville: Broadman Press, 1942.
McBeth, H. Leon. *The Baptist Heritage: Four Centuries of Baptist Witness.* Nashville: Broadman Press, 1987.
Nettles, Tom J. *The Oral Memoirs of Robert A. Baker.* Dallas: Baptist General Convention of Texas, 1981.
Price, J. M., ed. *Southwestern Men and Their Messages.* Kansas City: Central Seminary Press, 1948.
———. *Ten Men From Baylor.* Kansas City: Central Seminary Press, 1945.
Riley, B. F. *History of the Baptists of Texas.* Dallas: By the author, 1907.
Shurden, Walter B. *Not a Silent People: Controversies that have Shaped Southern Baptists.* Nashville: Broadman Press, 1972.

Articles

Allison, B. Gray. "Notable Achievements in Missions and Evangelism Since 1845." *Baptist History and Heritage* 24 (July 1989): 32-39.

Austin, James L. "How the Cooperative Program Developed." *Baptist History and Heritage* 17 (October 1982): 41-42.
Baker, Robert A. "The Cooperative Program in Historical Perspective." *Baptist History and Heritage* 10 (July 1975): 169-176.
Baptist Standard. 1908-1945.
Beck, Rosalie. "Lee Rutland Scarborough." *The Journal of Texas Baptist History* 1 (1981): 60-62.
Carter, James E. "The Fraternal Address of Southern Baptists." *Baptist History and Heritage* 12 (October 1977): 211-218.
———. "Southern Baptists' First Confession of Faith." *Baptist History and Heritage* 5 (January 1970): 24-28.
Dawson, J. M. "Along the Battle Front." *Baptist Standard,* 5 October 1922, 16-17.
Encyclopedia of Southern Baptists, 1958 ed. S.v. "Scarborough, Lee Rutland."
George, Timothy. "The Southern Baptist Cooperative Program: Heritage and Challenge." *Baptist History and Heritage* 20 (April 1985): 4-13.
Hobbs, Herschel H. "The Baptist Faith and Message – Anchored but Free." *Baptist History and Heritage* 13 (July 1978): 33-40.
Maston, T. B., ed. "Doctor Scarborough Memorialized." *Southwestern News* 3 (May 1945): 1-8.
McClellan, Albert. "The Shaping of the Southern Baptist Mind." *Baptist History and Heritage* 13 (July 1978): 2-11.
———. "Bold Mission Thrust of Baptists: Past and Present." *Baptist History and Heritage* 14 (January 1979): 3-15.
"Messengers Ask Dr. Norris to Explain 'Deacon Power.'" *World-Wide News,* 13 October 1922.
Mullins, E. Y. "Southern Baptists Concerned About Fundamentalist Invasion." *The Baptist,* 7 October 1922, 1111-1112.
Routh, E. C. "Things are Getting Better." *Baptist Standard,* 12 October, 1922, 8.

Unpublished

Baptist Biography File, Archives, A. Webb Roberts Library, Southwestern Baptist Theological Seminary, Fort Worth, Texas. S.v. "Scarborough, L. R."
Ray, Jefferson Davis. "The First Faculty of the Seminary." A Paper Presented for the Fortieth Anniversary of Southwestern Baptist Theological Seminary, 8 May 1948. Archives, A. Webb Roberts Library, Southwestern Baptist Theological Seminary, Fort Worth, Texas.
"Twenty-Fifth Anniversary Celebration of the Presidency of Dr. Scarborough." Archives, A. Webb Roberts Library, Southwestern Baptist Theological Seminary, Fort Worth, Texas.

Reference

Encyclopedia of Southern Baptists. 2 vols. Nashville: Broadman Press, 1958.
Noll, Mark A., ed. *Eerdmans' Handbook to Christianity in America.* Grand Rapids: William B. Eerdmans Publishing Co., 1983.
Schwarz, J. C., ed. *Who's Who in the Clergy, 1935-36.* New York: By the Author, 277 Broadway, 1936.

Bibliography

Starr, Edward C., ed. *A Baptist Bibliography: Being a Register of Printed Material by and about Baptists; Including Works Written Against Baptists.* 6 vols. Philadelphia: Judson Press, 1947.

Sound Recordings

Baker, Robert A. *History and Influence of Southwestern Baptist Theological Seminary: A Multimedia Presentation.* Fort Worth: Southwestern Baptist Theological Seminary, 1978. Cassette TC 5463.

Baptist Voices of Yesterday. Waco: Word, (197?). Cassette TC 1425.

Pamphlets

Miles, Delos. "L. R. Scarborough: Shaper of Evangelism," in *Shapers of Southern Baptist Heritage* (Nashville: The Historical Commission of the Southern Baptist Convention, 1987).

Index

A
Abilene, Texas, 4, 16-20
Anson, Texas, 4, 9, 12
Article 19 on Co-operation, 76
Atlanta, Georgia, 54

B
Baker, Robert A., 24, 38, 41
Baptist General Convention of Texas, 23, 34, 37, 44, 47, 51, 65, 71, 106
Baptist Standard, 67, 69
Baptist World Alliance, 106, 108
Barnard Hall, 40
Barnes, W. W., 41, 43, 50, 54, 102, 125
Barton, A. J., 55
Baylor Theological Seminary, 24
Baylor University, 6, 9, 10, 18, 23-24, 33, 43-44, 104
Big Spring, Texas, 4
Bottoms, G. W., 39
Broadway Baptist in Fort Worth, 67
Brooks, S. P., 24, 33, 43-44, 115-116, 127-128, 129
Buckner Orphanage, 27, 39
Burkhalter, Frank, 71

C
Cameron, Texas, 14-16
Campaign Commission, 55-58, 67, 68, 69, 77, 78
Carey, E. H., 129
Carroll, B. H., 4, 10, 12, 13, 20, 22, 23-32, 39, 43, 50, 80, 81, 82, 83, 89, 94, 101, 103-104, 105, 112, 124
Carter, Flora Mills, 39
Carver, W. O., 12
Clear Fork Creek, 9
Colfax, Louisiana, 2
Committee on Baptist Faith and Message, 75
Committee on Co-operation, 53-54
Committee on Financial Aspects, 55
Confederate Army, 2
Conservation Commission, 70-72, 85
Cooper, Oscar H., 18, 23
Cowden, George E., 38
  Mrs. George E., 38
Cowden Hall, 38

D
Dana, H. E., x, 18, 26, 42, 72, 103
Dow, Samuel, 43, 44
Durham, Supt., 129-130

E
Education Board, 46
Education Commission, 55
Endued to Win, 95, 96-97
Enlistment Month, 64-65
Erisophian Literary Society, 10
"Evangelism-Enlightenment-Enlistment," 62
evolution, 43-44, 113, 116, 127
Executive Committee of the Southern Baptist Convention, 54, 67, 77

F
"Facing a Worthy Task in a Worthy Way," 62
First Baptist Church in Abilene, 14, 16-20, 30
First Baptist Church in Atlanta, 56
First Baptist Church in Cameron, 14-16
First Baptist Church in Dallas, 27, 56
First Baptist Church in Fort Worth, 27, 42
First Baptist Church in McKinney, 65-66
First Baptist Church in Nashville, 58
First Baptist Church in Waco, 10, 20, 23, 44, 47-48, 104
Foreign Mission Board, 45-46, 53, 71, 93

Fort Worth Hall, 36
Frost, J. M., 30
Future Program Commission, 76-77

G
Gambrell, J. B., 24, 54, 62, 124
Gates, I. E., 65
Goodspeed, Calvin, 24
Gormley, J. W., 125-126
Green, D. F., 63
Greenwood Cemetery, 50
Groner, F. S., 65-66, 129
Gross, J. L., 84

H
Hamilton, William Wister, 82
Hanks, R. T., 5
Hardin-Simmons University, 18
Hening, B. C., 58, 68
Hog Creek Schoolhouse, 9
Holy Places and Precious Promises, xi
Home Mission Board, 46, 53, 72, 82, 83, 84, 93, 101, 107
Hot Springs, Arkansas, 82
Hundred Thousand Club, 39

I
Information Month, 64
Intercession Month, 64
Interchurch World Movement, 52

J
Jenkins, Millard, 68
Jones County, Texas, 3, 6, 9

L
Lee Rutland Scarborough: A Life of Service, x
Leggett, K. K., 9

M
McCart, H. C., 38, 45
McConnell, F. M., 126, 128
McDaniel, George W., 68
McDaniel Resolution, 128
McLennan County, Texas, 3, 4, 9
Macon, Georgia, 67
McPherson, G. W., 116
Marvels of Divine Leadership, 74, 81-82
Merkel, Texas, 8, 9, 12
Meroney, Prof., 125, 127

Millions for the Master, 61
Modern School of the Prophets, A, xi
Moore, Hight C., 58
Mullins, E. Y., 12, 30, 33

N
Nashville, Tennessee, 58
Neal, T. V., 61
Neel, Mrs. W. J., 58
New Denominationalism, ix-x, xi-xii, 51, 53, 59, 73-76, 78, 79, 80-82, 84, 88, 94, 97, 101, 106-109
New Hampshire Articles of Faith, 112
Newman, A. H., 24, 31
Norris, J. Frank, xi, 23, 42-50, 106, 112, 115-119, 120-132
Norrisism, 48-49, 51

O
O'Connell, Charles, 126

P
Phi Beta Kappa, 12
Pine Bluff, Arkansas, 26
Prepare to Meet God, xi

R
Ray, Jeff D., 25, 26, 76
  T. B., 59, 62
Recruits for World Conquests, x, 65, 85
Reeve, J. J., 31
Reynolds, I. E., 61-62
Riley, W. B., 30
Robertson, A. T., 12
Routh, E. C., 69
Rutland, W. R., 2

S
Sampey, J. R., 12
Scarborough, Emma, 9
  Eugenia, 2
  George Adolphus, 12
  George Warren, x, 1-7, 8, 10, 13, 14, 16, 20, 104
  Lee Rutland: baptism of, 12-13; birth of, 1-2; books about, x-xi; books by, xi, 65, 74, 81-82, 85-86, 87, 94-97, 100, 101, 107-108; boyhood of, ix, 1-8, 20;

Index

calls "the called," xii, 60, 65, 81, 82, 83–84, 85–88, 107; called to ministry, 13–14; conflict with J. Frank Norris, 42–51; as cowboy, 7–8; children of, 16; as chairman of Conservation Commission, 69–72, 85; death of, 102; education of, 6, 7, 8–12, 13–14, 20, 104; as evangelism professor, x, 22–23, 25–28, 31, 81, 83–101, 102; as evangelist, xi, xii, 22–23, 30, 69, 79, 80–101, 107; first sermon delivered by, 14; as fund-raiser, 18, 28, 35–41, 50, 53, 55–73, 75, 78, 107; interest in law, 9–12; invests personal funds, 37–38; land bought by, 44–45; marriage of, 15; New Denominationalism inspired by, *see* New Denominationalism; as pastor (Cameron), 14–16; (Abilene), 16–20, 30; as president of Southwestern, ix, xii, 22, 31–51, 57, 70, 81; resigns as president, Southwestern, 41–42; and 75 Million Campaign, ix, xii, 43, 45–46, 50, 52–79, 80–81, 82, 100, 106, 107
 Martha Elizabeth Rutland, 1–3, 5–7, 9, 10, 13, 20, 104
 Mary (Neppie), 15–16
 Nancy, 2
Seminary Hill, 22, 28–29
Seminary Hill Street Railway Company, 37–38
75 Million Campaign, ix, 45–46, 52–79, 80, 84, 107, 108, 130
Simmons College, 18, 20, 38, 57
Soda Water, Cigars and Campaign Pledges, 63
Southern Baptist Convention, xi, xii, 23, 34–35, 39, 43, 46, 52, 53–70, 68, 72, 73, 76, 78–79, 80, 82, 83, 84, 87, 106, 107, 108–109
Southern Baptist Cooperative Program, ix, 53, 76–77, 79, 107, 108

Southern Baptist Theological Seminary, 12, 20, 33
Southside Baptist in Birmingham, Alabama, 67
Southwestern Baptist Theological Seminary: books about, xi; debt incurred by, 36–39; early development, 22–34; fruit orchard owned by, 39; transfer of ownership, 34–35, 105
Spring Bible Conference, 30
Stewardship Month, 65
Sumner, Prof., 127
Sunday School Board, 58, 65

T
Tarrant Baptist Association, 35, 43, 44, 47, 49, 51, 116, 121–122, 123, 124, 128, 131
Texas Baptist Convention, 32
Thomas, Cullen F., 126–127
Thompson, C. M., 116
Truby Mound, Texas, 3, 9
Truett, George W., 56, 57–58, 68, 78

V
Van Ness, I. J., 58
Victory Week, 58, 66–67, 68
"Vital Discussion Between Two Business Men, A," 63

W
Warren, Mary P. (Neppie) (*see* Scarborough, Mary (Neppie))
"What You Have Missed," 70
"When Millions Come Pouring In," 61
Williams, Charles B., 25
Winston, J. K., 38
With Christ After the Lost, 95
Woman's Missionary Training School, 40
Woman's Missionary Union (WMU), 58, 59, 64

Y
Yale University, 12, 13, 104